ENDORSEMENTS

Like an Old Testament prophet, the bugle of warning to his lips, Ron Luce sounds the alarm for a generation at the crossroads. Even more importantly, he outlines a battle plan that is actually doable. Urgency and practicality in the same book . . . what a novel approach!

Mark Rutland, Ph.D., President
Oral Roberts University

Ron Luce's new book, *Double Vision*, is powerful, practical and packed with dynamic ideas for today's youth ministry. Don't miss this exciting new look at how to impact today's teens for Christ. No one does it better than Ron Luce and the people at Teen Mania.

Dr. Jerry Falwell, Founder
Liberty University

Ron Luce has taken youth ministry to the next level in his latest book. *Double Vision* offers a fresh look at new ways of reaching out to today's young people. It equips those engaged in youth ministry to break free of the status quo and do something significant with everlasting consequences. This book challenges us to greatness in our own walk and relationship with Christ. It provides step-by-step practical guidance on what to do and how to do it. This book will be an extremely valuable resource not only in your library but in your life and ministry. I highly recommend it to you.

Dr. Les Christie, Chair, Youth Ministry Department
William Jessup University, Rocklin, CA

DOUBLE VISION

– BEING THE LEADER OF A HIGH IMPACT YOUTH MINISTRY –

RONLUCE

Double Vision — Being the Leader of a High Impact Youth Ministry
Published by TM Publishing, a division of Teen Mania Ministries
22392 FM 16 West Garden Valley, TX 75771
www.teenmania.org

ISBN 978-1-936417-05-6
© 2010 Ron Luce

Printed in the United States of America

RELIGION / CHRISTIAN MINISTRY / YOUTH

DEDICATION

This book is dedicated to those who have poured their guts out for this generation.

ACKNOWLEDGMENTS

The Double Vision book series is the effort of many people's time and energy. I would like to acknowledge a few of those individuals.

Thank you to my Executive Team, Beth Powell, Rebekah Morris, Emily Johnson, Heidi Abigt, Laurie Fields, and LauRen Spillers. Thank you for all the work you do to keep things flowing and for all the hours that you put into making this book possible.

This book series would be meaningless without all the Youth Pastors and Youth Workers in the world. If you are a Youth Pastor or Youth Worker, I want to thank you for the time, blood, sweat, tears, and pizza you have gone through to reach this generation.

I have to acknowledge my amazing children Hannah, Charity, and Cameron. My wife of over 25 years, Katie, you are a wonderful wife, mother, and best friend.

Finally, John 15:5 says, *"I am the vine, you are the branches. . . without Me you can do nothing"* (NKJV). My life is nothing without the Lord. There aren't enough words in all the books in all the world to express how thankful I am to You.

CONTENTS

Dear Youth Leader,

We are in the middle of a battle for the hearts of a whole generation. If you are like most youth leaders in America, you are in the trenches every day. You're wearing yourself out trying to do whatever you can to love kids, lead them to Christ, and help them grow. Even with all that's done in the name of youth ministry, we are still losing a generation. It seems like the media and the enemy have been working harder than we have. They are destroying a generation at a faster rate than we are rescuing it. At current rates of evangelism, only four percent of this generation will be Bible-believing Christian adults. If we continue doing youth ministry the way we have been, we will end up with an America unlike any we have ever known. Something has to change!

What you have in your hands is more than a book series. This is a manual to provoke a revolution in communities, churches, and youth ministries across America. If we want to capture the heart of this generation before it's too late, we need thousands of youth ministries and groups to double and disciple every year. *Double Vision* will help you to build a thriving, solid youth ministry that continues to flourish and grow without burning you out.

This book series and its accompanying CD-ROM are embedded with proven strategies and principles for building a thriving youth ministry. Already, thousands of youth pastors across the country are seeing God work powerfully through these new paradigms!

I encourage you to begin to dream God's dream for you in youth ministry. Could you be one of the 100,000 youth groups needed to capture the hearts of this generation? I believe if we all throw our hearts into this, work hard, work smart, and ask the Holy Spirit to guide us, we can win this war! We need to have drastic change . . . it has to start now . . . it has to start with us.

I look forward to laboring with you and thousands of other youth pastors of every denomination and background. I believe we will see a miracle in the hearts of this generation!

Consumed by the Call,

Ron Luce

President and Founder
Teen Mania Ministries

INTRODUCTION

You have in your hands a document of war—a blueprint for strategic thinking about your local youth ministry. It is meant to help you launch a local offensive in your region to rescue teens caught in the middle of the current war for their hearts and minds. It is meant to provoke a revolution in youth ministry.

We must come to grips with the fact that—in spite of all of our best efforts to minister to young people—we are on the brink of losing a generation! The world and the enemy have been working harder, investing millions, and gaining more ground than we have. We cannot simply do more of the same old things and hope to turn this generation around. We must change what we are doing. We must change how we think about youth ministry before it is too late.

What do I mean by too late? First, consider the numbers: the millennial generation is the largest and richest generation in American history. Every year, 4.5 million American teenagers turn 20, and research shows that the odds against someone turning to Christ after reaching this milestone are significant. (We know that 77 percent of people who receive Christ do so before they are 21 years old). At the present rate of evangelism, only four percent of this generation will be Bible-believing—so we must act NOW to prevent them from going into their adult years as unbelievers.[1] Our passion is fueled by the fact that in five to seven years MOST of this generation will be in their 20s. NOW is the time to capture their hearts.

With the urgency of the moment fresh in our minds, let us approach youth ministry with a new perspective. It is time to shift our focus off of maintaining ministry the way it's always been done—the weekly meetings, our regular programs, ski trips and bake sales. What will capture the critical mass of the youth in any region is a vision-driven, not program-driven, local youth ministry. And that is where you come in!

Those of us engaged in youth ministry need to redefine our job descriptions. In this war for today's generation, we are the generals. Wars are won by the generals in the field, and those generals must have a plan to win each battle. That is what this book is all about—a new paradigm that leads to a different kind of planning and a new way of executing local youth ministry.

Don't be intimidated by the size of this book series, or get weary in the planning process. You are invited to use the text of this guide with the included CD-ROM as a tool for the battle-planning process. These steps are the work of generals that are determined to win. Let us all commit ourselves to becoming generals.

1. The Barna Group, "Research Shows that Spiritual Maturity Process Should Start at a Young Age," (November 17, 2003) ttp://www.barna.org/FlexPage.aspx?Page=BarnaUpdate&BarnaUpdateID=153

CHAPTER ONE

Keeping Your Spiritual Edge

Have you ever noticed that once in a while when you hear someone preach, you are so moved and so inspired that you want to jump up and shout amen! Or you want to fall on your knees and cry out to God with all your heart! You may have heard others preach on that same Scripture passage, but it never really came alive before—there was no bite, no thunder. How is it that it's easy to walk away from one speaker untouched, while someone else pours life into your soul and compels you to respond in repentance? The answer is the power of the edge.

You can tell when *the edge* is there and when it isn't. Some Christian musicians have it, and you can't help but weep when you hear their music. Others never have it; and

As Youth Specialists, we need to make sure that our ministry is potent.

some have it, but lose it. What exactly is *the edge* in ministry, and how do you make sure you have it and never lose it?

Many youth leaders demonstrate good teaching skills but have no real fire, and that disturbs me. It ought to disturb us all. As Youth Specialists, we need to make sure that our ministry is potent. If we are going to spend our energy in the trenches fighting for this generation and if we are to make a real impact in teens' lives we'd better fully understand this.

Let's begin by looking at what the edge is *not*. You know you've lost your edge when "pretty good" ministry is good enough, when you think you can do the work and programs of the ministry without the Lord, and when your involvement in ministry doesn't personally challenge you to press deeper into the things of God. In short, you know you've lost your edge:

- when you have **programs** without a **product**;
- when you have vast **resources** without **results**;
- when you have **preaching**, but you have no **passion**;
- when you go through **motions** but provide no real **ministry**;
- when you have many **services** but no Spirit;
- when you issue a **challenge**, but there's no **conviction**;
- when you display **emotion**, but it sounds **empty**.

Well then, what is the edge? For one thing, it's sheer *determination.*

Jacob had the edge. He had the edge when he wrestled with the "man" (God) in the desert: "Then the man said, 'Let me go, for it is daybreak.' But Jacob replied, 'I will not let you go unless you bless me'" (Gen. 32:26).

What determination! When you've got the edge, you have a *determination* to find God and to obtain His blessing. Jacob had that edge: "You're not going anywhere until I have your blessing and feel your presence transforming me way down deep in my being." Today's Youth Specialist might say it like this: "Lord, don't let me go through the motions of this quiet time (or this youth meeting, or this counseling session, or this fun night, or this sermon) without touching my life and touching others through me with Your fire. I *must* have the edge!" Do you have that Jacob-like determination?

Moses had the edge. He had the edge the very first time he looked Pharaoh in the eye and said, "Let my people go!" (You do NOT say that to Pharaoh unless you have some confidence in your God.) The edge also means having the *confidence* to make a demand on behalf of God. Moses had the audacity to make a demand because he knew the Almighty Lord would back him up. When you've got the edge, you can make a demand. It doesn't mean you go through life ordering everyone around. But you're confident enough to demand that the devil leave and to pray with more than hot air. Do you have Moses-like confidence?

Jeremiah had the edge. He had the edge when he realized: "But if I say, 'I will not mention him or speak any more in his name,' his word is in my heart like a fire, fire shut up in my bones. I am weary of holding it in; indeed, I cannot" (Jer. 20:9).

If you have a word burning in your heart, you can't keep it to yourself. That's the edge.

The edge means having a *fire* you can't keep down. The prophet proclaims, "I've got to say something about this. It's on fire inside of me. I cannot shut up!" When you've got the edge, you've got fire. If you have a word burning in your heart, you can't keep it to yourself. That's the edge: determination, confidence, fire. What else is it?

Elijah had the edge. He had the edge when he called fire down from heaven. He did not care about the trends of society—that so many others were worshiping Baal. He knew God would answer him and prove himself strong. When you have your edge you have a *backbone* like Elijah to stand against all the social norms that are ungodly.

John the Baptist had the edge. He had the edge when he said: "You are a brood of vipers. Show me the fruit of your repentance!" When you have your edge you can stand strong and not worry about what anyone thinks of you! You know you are clean, and are bold about pointing out compromises.

Peter had the edge. He had the edge when he looked at the crowd and said to the very people who had killed Christ, "But you crucified the Lord of Glory . . ." Their response was to ask, "What can we do to be saved?" When you have your edge you *compel people* with your heartfelt words and they come running to Christ! (In Peter's case, they didn't even wait for an altar call; they interrupted him before he was done!)

HOW DO I LOSE MY EDGE?

Here's the answer in a word: sin. Big sin. Small sin. Public sin. Secret sin. Compromises of all sizes will cost you your edge. If you have been convicted by God about an area of your life, and you persist in going against what you know is right, your edge starts to dull. You slip up in an area, slip up again, and then it becomes a regular part of your lifestyle. You keep "doing the work of the ministry," but it loses its potency.

HOW DO I GET MY EDGE BACK?

Here's another one-word answer: repent. Get rid of that sin. Turn your back on that small compromise that no one would really know about. God demands more of a leader. A leader cannot say, "Well, *others* do it!" If God has convicted you, then you need to do what HE is telling you to do. Go on a fast. Get away from the world. Return to your first love! Don't be content with "pretty good is good enough" ministry.

Sad to say, I have seen ministers who—after a massive moral failure—never got their original edge back. I know they are forgiven, and they know it, but somehow they "walk with a limp" the rest of their lives. So guard your edge, and don't take it lightly! It is the precious ministry of God to a dying world in all its full-blown potency.

HOW CAN I SHARPEN MY EDGE ONCE I'VE GOT IT?

This is the question every Youth Specialist ought to ask him or herself every day. I believe it initially involves making *three distinct changes* in your approach to ministry. You must move:

. . . *from memories to present reality.* It is natural for people to live from experience to experience. Who doesn't like to recall the "mountaintop" experiences with God and long to relive them again? But there's a better way.

Remember what Paul said to Timothy: "Fan into flame the gift of God, which is in you through the laying on of my hands" (2 Tim. 1:6).

Even Timothy had to be reminded to keep the fire burning. Our goal is not just an experience with God that we can remember and then try to repeat, over and over again. Our goal is not to simply sing about the day, 10 years ago, when God showed up and brought deep conviction so we can preach about it again, remembering, "Wasn't that an exciting day?"

Don't fall into the trap of building your theology and program around that one radical experience you had with God in the past. If reproducing a memory is your goal, you will pray this way: "Oh, God, rain your fire down again; give us another experience like the one burning in our memories." Instead, God calls us to consider *today*. He wants us to pray not just for an experience of revival, but for an entire lifestyle of glory. Do you see the difference? If we would stay "vived," we would not need to be "re-vived."

. . . from relightings to fanning. Even after a real encounter with God, *it only takes about 24 hours for your relationship with God to go stale.* Here's how it happens: You have a wonderful meeting, filled with God's presence. You have some great music, you're on a spiritual high, and it all happened after that one song. So you say, "We are definitely going to sing that song again." You assume the answer is in the song.

But the song isn't what brings the fire—God alone brings the fire.

Another time you pray, and kids are convicted. Next time, you think: "I will pray just like that again." You hope to relight what was once on fire. But the prayer isn't what brings the fire either—God brings it.

Rather than looking for a formula for fire, suppose we maintain a glowing inner fervor that will not die? You see, you are a man, a woman, from another world. People don't know what you know. They have not experienced what you have, because you have spent so much more time with God. You have a deep reservoir, a raging fire burning within you. God's glory shines in your eyes, glows through your entire lifestyle, and emerges for all to see. So when you stand to preach, you've got the edge.

Have you ever tried to light the coals for a barbecue using lighter fluid? I used to think that if I flooded the coals, the fire would burn; so I'd light it and leave. Ten minutes later I would return and it would be out. I would repeat the first step again. Then out it would go again. This looks like a lot of people in church today. Just "hoping one day it will stick." God wants to blow on us with His Spirit—like I learned to blow on those coals until they were bright orange. Rather than seeking to relight the fire, why ever let it go out? Go for the glow. Fan the fire, day in and day out. It's about who you *are* in Christ, not what you *do* next.

Fan it, fan it, until your normal walk is a bright glow of raging fire and passion for Him alone.

. . . from explosions to essence. On our very first mission trip in 1987, we went to a place where two volcanic mountain peaks sat side by side. One was an active volcano and one was inactive. I hiked with 60 teenagers to the top of the inactive peak, hoping that from there we could look down into the active volcano and see the fiery lava, bubbling and shooting up into the air.

Instead, we saw fog. The peak we stood upon was

God alone
brings the fire.

Go for the glow. Fan the fire, day in and day out. It's about who you are in Christ, not what you do next.

much higher, shrouded in the clouds. I just could not resist so I decided to hike over to the active peak, go up to the edge and look down. This was dangerous, but I took the risk. (I don't recommend doing this!)

I thought I would look down into the red-hot, boiling lava; instead, I saw some little glowing holes in a hard cap of stone. Every once in a while we'd hear the sound of explosions, so I decided to try to capture the moment on film. There was one picture left in my camera, and when I heard the next "pop," I snapped the shot. To my amazement, I captured little pieces of orange-glowing lava hanging in mid-air—an awesome display bursting out of dismal smog.

That is what we hope for in ministry, right? That little explosion. We just can't wait for the next pop. The real goal, though, is to have hearts of raging lava. The little bit that comes out of the top when you minister is nothing compared to all that lava, that stuff God is doing within you, forming you to be like Christ. That work is the fire raging deep in your soul. It is the very essence of your life, this relationship with the Almighty. This is what we're after—the glow of the deep fire of God. Not just hype, not just excitement, not just an experience. A lifestyle.

ENJOY CREATIVE TIMES WITH GOD

I'm sure you've realized by now that the changes above are really one movement described in three different ways. The crucial question is, have you made the switch? If so, you can keep fanning the coals of the fire. It's a matter of spending time with God, and I believe He calls us to be very creative with Him in this relationship.

"But, Ron, how can I have creative times with God?" I'm glad you asked! Here are some ways:

Expand your prayer plan. Don't just pray for the same old thing by going down the same tired prayer list. For example, suppose you were to pray for some things that have no beneficial bearing on your own ministry? Could you intercede for someone else's ministry, someone else's youth group, someone else's church, or someone else's financial problems?

And isn't prayer more than just asking for things? Perhaps it is a time to get to know God, time to let Him stir you up a bit as you spend silent moments listening to Him for a change. Let Him stir up your heart for what He cares about—other people's ministries, missionaries you have never met before, other ministries you don't know much about (but you have a newsletter and see a need, so you pray).

Larry Lea came to speak to our staff and interns a year ago and said, "The most important thing in prayer is that you *connect with God.*" You don't have to remember all of the missionaries around the world . . . but at least connect.

Freshen up your worship. King David urged God's people: "Enter his gates with thanksgiving and his courts

This is what we're after—the glow of the deep fire of God. Not just hype, not just excitement, not just an experience. A lifestyle.

Isn't prayer more than just asking for things? Perhaps it is a time to get to know God, time to let Him stir you up a bit as you spend silent moments listening to Him for a change.

with praise; give thanks to him and praise his name" (Ps. 100:4). There is only one way to enter into the courts of the Lord, and that is with thanksgiving and praise. You can scream it, you can shout it, you can talk it, but there is only one way to get in.

Before Jesus came, the blood of sacrificial animals was payment for the high priest's entry into the Holy of Holies. But now . . .

> It is impossible for the blood of bulls and goats to take away sins.
>
> Therefore, when Christ came into the world, he said: "Sacrifice and offering you did not desire, but a body you prepared for me; with burnt offerings and sin offerings you were not pleased. Then I said, 'Here I am—it is written about me in the scroll—I have come to do your will, O God.'" . . .
>
> And by that will, we have been made holy through the sacrifice of the body of Jesus Christ once for all.
>
> Day after day every priest stands and performs his religious duties; again and again he offers the same sacrifices, which can never take away sins. But when this priest had offered for all time one sacrifice for sins, he sat down at the right hand of God. . . .
>
> Therefore, brothers, since we have confidence to enter the Most Holy Place by the blood of Jesus, by a new

and living way opened for us through the curtain, that is, his body, and since we have a great priest over the house of God, let us draw near to God with a sincere heart in full assurance of faith, having our hearts sprinkled to cleanse us from a guilty conscience and having our bodies washed with pure water.
—Hebrews 10:4–7, 10–12, 19–22

Don't kill anything; Jesus paid the price. The only thing left to give, then, is thanks and praise, the fruit of our lips. That opens doors.

Here's a creative approach I like to use: open your Bible and read one or two Psalms as if you had written them. Think about what David had in mind when he wrote, "As the deer pants for streams of water, so my soul pants for you, O God" (Ps. 42:1). Then say it over and over so that it becomes your own heart cry. "Yes, God, as the deer pants, so *my* soul longs for You!"

Thankfully, the Bible pictures the worship taking place in heaven. Let it move you into fresh and creative means of praise:

At once I was in the Spirit, and there before me was a throne in heaven with someone sitting on it. And the one who sat there had the appearance of jasper and carnelian. A rainbow, resembling an emerald, encircled the throne. Surrounding the throne were twenty-four other thrones, and seated on them were twenty-four elders. They were dressed in white and had crowns of gold on their heads. From the throne came flashes of lightning, rumblings and peals of thunder. Before the throne, seven lamps were blazing. These are the seven spirits of God. Also before the throne there was what looked like a sea of glass, clear as crystal.

In the center, around the throne, were four living creatures, and they were covered with eyes, in front and in back. The first living creature was like a lion, the second was like an ox, the third had a face like a man, the fourth was like a flying eagle. Each of the four living creatures had six wings and was covered with eyes all around, even under his wings. Day and night they never stop saying: "Holy, holy, holy is the Lord God Almighty, who was, and is, and is to come." Whenever the living creatures give glory, honor and thanks to him who sits on the throne and who lives for ever and ever, the twenty-four elders fall down before him who sits on the throne, and worship him who lives for ever and ever. They lay their crowns before the throne and say: "You are worthy, our Lord and God, to receive glory and honor and power, for you created all things, and by your will they were created and have their being."

—Revelation 4:2–11

The 24/7 elders are so stunned by God's presence that they cannot even stand up. They bow and say, "Holy, holy, holy," for the first million years and then the next million years. Can we be stunned by His presence for even a few moments? Creative worship means never singing a song just for the sake of singing a song, never letting it come off our lips without coming from a heart that is bowled over with God's majesty and goodness toward us. His grace truly is stunning—worthy of all praise for a billion years.

Color your readings with creativity. Bible reading is a primary means of spiritual growth, and it, too, can be done creatively to keep the fires burning. For example, try studying by theme, finding out all about forgiveness, or fellowship, or God's sovereignty, or church disciplines, etc.

Or approach Scripture through memorization for a while. As you memorize, you are meditating upon God's Word and His will—and that's a good thing! Now you have a little more revelation, a little more truth burning inside of you.

Or try biographical reading, studying Bible characters' lives. Find out everything you can about David, or Timothy, or Barnabas, or Paul. What can you learn from them about how to love and obey God? What warnings or cautions come through as you study their sins and mistakes? Such study fans the flames.

As you read the Scripture creatively, always look for the character of God. Do you know what He is like? For as you dive into the Scriptures, you enter a quest to know God. And as you explore, determine never to read a chapter in the Bible without thinking, "God, give me some of your character. Explain to me a little more of what You are like. Lord, feed me. I want to know You."

Getting to know Him means recognizing His match-less character all through the Scripture, Old Testament and New. "Why did you put that rule there, Lord? What about that commandment? Why did you act that way?" Think about what He did, why He did it, what He said, when He said it, and to whom He said it. "What does this tell me about You? For You are the One I want to know better and better." He reveals Himself right here. His character is written all over the pages of your Bible. So read creatively, and look for God's character in every chapter.

Calendar-ize your seasons of solitude. I am not talking about moments with God in the morning; I am talking about getting creative with your time by planning whole seasons alone with Him. Why not enter those seasons on your calendar months in advance?

This doesn't mean you have to live up in the hills like a monk. You can be alone and still have your normal lifestyle. But I suggest you get rid of some things. Could you turn off the music? Unplug the television set? Stop the

Read the Scripture creatively, always look for the character of God.

newspaper deliveries for a while? Just take the next season—one week, two weeks, or more—to be alone. You can be around people, but you don't have to be around the noise of the world.

It might well call for physical solitude, though. And for most of us it will feel awkward at first. We'll keep wondering, "What am I supposed to be *doing*?" Until we realize that God is calling us to stop doing for awhile; He is calling us just to BE. With Him.

We have this idea that "the anointing" is some magic thing that we ought to pray for right before we preach. But no, it is not this mystical little help that God gives us. The anointing forms, over time, by your time alone. Get alone *with* God and get the anointing *from* God.

For the man or woman who comes to know and love God as Father in such intimacy, the times of solitude are the most exquisite in all of life. They are "a rendezvous with the Beloved." They are anticipated eagerly; awaited with acute expectancy; relished with enthusiasm. In a word, these times are highlights of life.

From W. Phillip Keller, *Men's Devotional Bible* (Grand Rapids: Zondervan, 1993)

Your preaching will never be more anointed than your quiet times are. If you don't have an anointed quiet time, don't expect to have a good sermon. Don't expect to have a good counseling session. That is where the anointing comes from. It is raging inside you, stirring your heart up.

You can worry that your relationship with [God] has gone cold, that you've lost your spiritual edge. You can think it will take a lot of time, a month or so of spiritual discipline, to get going again with Him. Then you sit down and discover, in just minutes, that you don't have to do a thing—except take some time. Be alone with Him. In what feels like no time you are caught up again in your love.

From Tim Stafford, *A Scruffy Husband Is a Happy Husband* (Colorado Springs: Focus on the Family, 1981)

Forget your food (for a while). Jesus said in Matthew 6, "*When* you fast . . ." In other words, He expected us to be doing this as a part of our lifestyle.

When you fast, do not look somber as the hypocrites do, for they disfigure their faces to show men they are fasting. I tell you the truth, they have received their reward in full. But when you fast, put oil on your head and wash your face, so that it will not be obvious to men that you are fasting, but only to your Father, who is unseen; and your Father, who sees what is done in secret, will reward you.

—Matthew 6:16–18

Oh, God, give me that reward! It says, don't let anybody know you're fasting. That is hard. You begin a fast for three days, and you already have several lunch appointments set up. Or maybe you plan to block out your schedule and somebody else schedules an appointment for you to go eat lunch with another (usually someone "important").

If you want to fast for a week or even a day, it won't be easy. You have to maneuver around the obstacles. But there is a reward that only comes when you fast. You separate yourself and say, "Lord, I don't want bread from this world,

Your ministry is a direct reflection of what's going on inside of you.

I want the Bread that comes from heaven. That is what I am going to feast on. Lord God, stir me up. I don't have any more energy to live in this world. I need some manna. Lord, I need some manna."

Fasting sharpens you. It humbles you and gets you crying out to God. Revelation comes your way, and Scriptures come alive with meaning like never before. Fasting is much more than just going hungry. It is giving your hungry heart to God.

THE BOTTOM LINE!

Everything we've been saying in this chapter boils down to one key point. So please listen closely, and take this to heart: *Your ministry is a direct reflection of what's going on inside of you.*

If you have your edge, and you are spiritually sharp, your ministry will cut deeply into human hearts and bring glory to God. If you have that raging fire in you, you'll be able to ignite other people. If you have the edge, it will show in your ministry.

Therefore, when you come to those times when you feel you just "can't seem to get through to the kids," look inside. You may conclude that the kids have hard hearts. But look inside. You've been preaching, you've been doing your meetings. You've been busy, but nothing's happening. Look inside.

Inside you are not living by your convictions and you have gotten dull. You have not really pressed through; you've forgotten how to be with God. Therefore the edge is dull, the fire has grown cold.

This is harsh, I know. But it is the truth. Groups take on the nature of their leader—or they leave. The people who stay have what you've got. If you have a raging fire, you make them hungry for it. You pass it on without even realizing it.

All the planning, organizing, and implementing we have talked about in the first half of this book are useless without your edge.

Now, stop everything and do whatever it takes to get your edge!

Fasting is much more than just going hungry. It is giving your hungry heart to God.

CHAPTER TWO

Watch Out for the Residue!

Time for a spin on the motorcycle! As I rolled it out of the garage into the sunlight, I noticed a little dust on the gas tank. No problem. I was soon zipping along the highway, expecting to leave any dust far behind in the wind. Not so. I looked down, and there it was—that thin, dusty coating defying a 60-mile-per-hour gale.

You can't find a much lighter substance on earth. You can barely touch it with your finger, yet it clings tenaciously to everything it encounters. That experience opened my eyes to something important about you and me: we easily lose our shine in the dust-laden atmosphere of our world.

We easily lose our shine in the dust-laden atmosphere of our world.

And we can't just blow it off.

The problem is, it's so easy to get along as a Christian and not have to deal with the layer of dust. After all, compared to somebody else (who's never been on a mission trip), we look pretty good. This dust that floats through our environment, however, the grime and residue of a fallen world, is the realm of "the ruler of the kingdom of the air" (Eph. 2:2). Satan himself is in charge of the dust. He's at home in it, and he'd like us to become quite comfortable with a little less spiritual sheen each day. Even if we are godly people, we live in an ungodly world; dust is flying everywhere.

It sticks to us with ease. Each of us could name hundreds of examples of how it happens. If you didn't see it live on TV a few years ago, then you probably saw a photo of that infamous kiss between Madonna and Britney. It's just one small example. You look at something like that and you are almost incredulous. You don't want to look . . . but then you do. And even though you don't want it to dust your mind, it immediately becomes a piece of lint landing ever-so-lightly in your consciousness. A piece of corruption from the world. You know it's not right, but those women look cool—and all of America just took a step down the staircase of what's "acceptable" in our society. As a result, some teenage boys now think it's cool to get their girlfriends to make out with one another. It really is okay, right? (Hey, we saw it on TV.) And why even mention the connection we now find between oral sex, junior-high girls, and Monica Lewinsky? It's not really sex, right? (Hey, we heard it on the radio.)

As Youth Specialists, we aren't in the ministry just so we can put on a few good programs. No, we want to rock the planet! Yet, if we look at past movements where God really "showed up," there was always a great cleansing revival filled with repentance, fasting, and seeking God with tearstained faces. How do we draw our kids into that kind of revolutionary, heart-wrenching longing for God? Instead of begging them to *please* come to church, what will it take to see them banging on the church doors because they *just can't stay away* from the Lord and His work among them?

I hate to say it. It's scary. But too many of us have gotten so used to having the residue of the world on us; we think it is normal. We walk around with a thin film of dust on us and don't even realize it, but then wonder why our ministry is not as potent as others. We must let the light of God shine on our souls so we can see the lint the world has deposited on us. Then we ask God to purify us from the accumulation of filth!

NO MORE DUST—ON ME

Let's take our eyes off the kids for a moment. We, as youth leaders, must stay dust free. This is the bottom line of all our ministry efforts.

"But Ron," you say. "Isn't it true that we need to really know our current youth culture? How can we do that

We must let the light of God shine on our souls so we can see the lint the world has deposited on us. Then we ask God to purify us from the accumulation of filth!

without immersing ourselves in it? We can't just stand out-side and observe, right?"

Wrong. Go ahead, prayerfully observe. Then, prayer-fully . . . *pray*. I'm tired of the excuse that says, "We need to relate to the world." So we go see all the movies, go visit all the bars, go dance at all the raves, and end up with a whole layer of dust on us. Soon we begin to think it's okay.

Have you ever sat in a room with the sunlight shining through in just the right way, so you could see every minute particle of dust in the air? At those moments you realize just how pervasive dust is. Even people who keep their houses "spotless" have to admit that a thin layer of dust covers everything. They can vacuum, but the vacuum cleaner won't catch it all; in fact, the vacuum blows much of it back into the air. That thin layer remains, in our homes and in our lives. Think about these two important things:

First, if we learn to tolerate a thin layer of dirt, in time we will gradually tolerate much, much more. Then, when we preach and teach and counsel, we won't have the fire at all; it will be a spark at best. Sadly, we'll think, "Well, the wind will blow it off, because I'm moving at a hectic pace, doing things for God. A little dust can't stand that kind of velocity." But it can. We live in a sinful world, and stuff is flying around us all the time. That's why, in my family, we hardly watch television any more—that's too much dust ready to settle into our minds.

Second, if we invite Jesus to invade our darkness, He will shine us up for effective ministry. We must constantly do this because we really won't see how the dust has affected us until we turn the lights up bright.

You were once darkness, but now you are light in the Lord. Live as children of light.

—Ephesians 5:8

I'm sure you've been to one of those car washes where the idea is to blow the dust off your car with a stream of water. I've found that I have to wipe the surfaces with a towel, though, if I really want it clean. It is the same way with our lives. As we start to feel the buildup of dust and corruption from the world—and the light comes in and we see it—then we have to let Jesus come right in and shine us up. How long has it been since you let Jesus shine you up?

The idea is to have nothing to do with the fruitless deeds of darkness. Jesus says, in effect, "I want to turn the light on and expose the dust particles in the culture and in your life."

HOW TO STAY DUST FREE

We took our kids to see the movie *Cheaper by the Dozen*. This was not an off-the-cuff decision. We had read several reviews (even from Christian Web sites). "It's so funny!" they all said.

So we took the kids to see it. And yes, it certainly has some funny parts. It also has some blatantly sinful parts. The producers know that thousands of young children will see the film, so I have to ask: why did they insert morally damaging aspects into a film when they could just as easily have stuck with harmless, traditional values?

Yet we Christians march our kids in to see it all. The Christian Web sites screening such films weren't even tuned in enough to say, "Don't go see this; you'll get dust on you and your children. You'll encounter values you're trying to get them to oppose. Stay home and talk or play a board game

As we start to feel the buildup of dust and corruption from the world—we have to let Jesus come right in and shine us up.

together. It's not worth the damage." But none of them said that. My children got a big piece of dust on them.

> *Therefore do not be partners with them.*
> *For you were once darkness, but now you are light in the Lord. Live as children of light (for the fruit of the light consists in all goodness, righteousness and truth) and find out what pleases the Lord. Have nothing to do with the fruitless deeds of darkness, but rather expose them. For it is shameful even to mention what the disobedient do in secret. But everything exposed by the light becomes visible, for it is light that makes everything visible. This is why it is said: "Wake up, O sleeper, rise from the dead, and Christ will shine on you."*
> *Be very careful, then, how you live—not as unwise but as wise, making the most of every opportunity, because the days are evil.*
> —Ephesians 5:7–16

The light makes everything visible. If we are going to call our youth to be radical Christians, then we also have to ask Jesus to do some work on us. I suggest five clues to keeping the residue of the world from attaching itself to you:

1. In prayer, ask to see the dust in your life. This is difficult! Which of us really wants to see all that internal grime for what it really is? Yet we must start with an honest prayer, "Jesus, let me see the dust; turn on the light. Don't let me get comfortable in a dusty life." We are simply asking to live a life that is content to know God, to hear His voice, to be led by His hand. Do we really need more? Here's another Scripture that speaks to this:

> *"Your eye is the lamp of your body. When your eyes are good, your whole body also is full of light. But when they are bad, your body also is full of darkness. See to it, then,*

that the light within you is not darkness. Therefore, if your whole body is full of light, and no part of it dark, it will be completely lighted, as when the light of a lamp shines on you."

—Luke 11:34–36

We get residue on our eyes—the lens into our soul—when we let dust settle on our conscience, our sensitivity to what is right and wrong. Then we're seeing through a glass that's much dimmer than it should be, and we can't see the things of God clearly. The Word of God doesn't make sense like it used to make sense. We can't hear His voice so well, and can't seem to discern His leading.

That's why we pray, "Lord, let me see that dust!"

Every once in a while, when I am praying, I get to see. It is humbling and humiliating. But it's also liberating when this happens, when that stroke of light comes from the Lord, and I have to admit: I can't *believe* I had that attitude. Now I see. I was so selfish. I am so embarrassed, because I see this big piece of lint that was invisible moments before.

I repent, and a little lint is wiped away.

Search me, O God, and know my heart; test me, and know my anxious thoughts. See if there is any offensive way in me, and lead me in the way everlasting.

—Psalm 139:23–24

Even though it is embarrassing, I would rather be humbled and deal with it. I get a raw glimpse of the flesh that still lives in me. I am me-centered, and I hate to remember that.

Jesus, let me see the dust; turn on the light.

The light makes everything visible. If we are going to call our youth to be radical Christians, then we also have to ask Jesus to do some work on us.

But it is the first step toward something better. *Lord, turn up the lights and let me see.*

2. Once you see it, name it, and bring it to God. We're not just talking about dust "in general." It's not enough to know you're a sinner "in principle." No, Christ calls you to come to Him with full knowledge of your need, and a no-nonsense recognition of just exactly what's in your heart.

In many cases, you never sought the dust. It was in the air; you thought it was one thing—you read the reviews— you moved toward it, and then it betrayed you.

Maybe you walk by a magazine and catch a glimpse of something pornographic. You walk away, but now you have this piece of lint on you. It just sort of happens. Maybe it's a television commercial that violates you. You never saw it before, but it "dusts" you pretty good. Bring that to God in a humble way, and respond to Him. "Lord, I feel like I have been violated. I need to be washed in the blood of Jesus. I need You to cleanse me of the thing that I did not invite."

There is dust everywhere, and it's bound to land on us now and then. Thankfully, we can walk under the shower of forgiveness—the waterfall of grace. God can clean us off again.

3. Expand the clean-up zone. If you're on a clean-up mission, you start with yourself but then you move out into a broader area. Do everything you can to protect your spouse and children, to create as much of a dust-free environment as possible.

You see, I don't think it's good enough to say, "We live in a dust-covered world, and we are going to get dust on us, and it's okay." No, I believe we must take preemptive action for ourselves *and on behalf of others*. The concept of Christian fellowship itself demands this. After all, we aren't Lone Ranger believers, even though we may be completely alone at any given moment. Here is what Dietrich Bonhoeffer, noted theologian and writer, had to say:

> *The individual must realize that his hours of aloneness react upon the community. In his solitude he can sunder and besmirch the fellowship, or he can strengthen and hallow it. Every act of self-control of the Christian is also a service to the fellowship.*
>
> *On the other hand, there is no sin in thought, word, or deed, no matter how personal or secret, that does not inflict injury upon the whole fellowship. An element of sickness gets into the body; perhaps nobody knows where it comes from or in what member it has lodged, but the body is infected. . . .*
>
> *We are members of a body, not only when we choose to be, but in our whole existence. Every member serves the whole body, either to its health or to its destruction. This is no mere theory; it is a spiritual reality. And the Christian community has often experienced its effects*

I am me-centered, and I hate to remember that. But it is the first step toward something better.

We are connected to one another in the
Body of Christ. What we do is done in
the body; what is done to me
happens to all of us.

*with disturbing clarity, sometimes destructively and
sometimes fortunately.*
From Dietrich Bonhoeffer, *Life Together* (San
Francisco: Harper & Row Publishers, Inc., 1954), 88-89.

We are connected to one another in the Body of Christ.
What we do is done in the body; what is done to me happens to all of us. My life in the Spirit is the life you live in the
same Spirit. We must protect ourselves in order to protect
one another.

We need to do things, then, that help insulate our
"environment"—which includes all of our relationships in
Christ. Therefore, again, ask Him to expose the dust that just
landed on you, a member of Christ's body. It's for
your good!

4. Stop inviting the dust to linger for "just a while."
Just because there are dust particles in the air, and they are
landing on me, doesn't mean it's okay for them to stay. That
is why the Bible says, "Wake up, O sleeper, rise from the
dead, and Christ will shine on you" (Eph. 5:14).

This is the embarrassing part, though, because what
happens to us is so subtle. For example, you're enjoying a
Seinfeld rerun, and it's genuinely funny. You can appreciate
it, because God made you with a sense of humor. What
you're watching is clearly innocent . . . until suddenly it

moves into perverted sexual humor. Do you leave it on or shut it off? Do you invite the lint to stay and camp out?

Or maybe you put a rented movie into your VCR or DVD player at home and before long the words and innuendos start getting explicit. If I'm watching with my wife Katie, she'll say, "Ron, I don't like this."

I'll put her off saying, "Honey, it's going to get better . . ."

"But Ron, I don't like this . . ."

"This is a really good part right here," I usually say. "It's getting better."

You've been there, right? Most of the time, it doesn't get a bit better. And there I am, covered in dust.

We aren't watching blatantly bad mass-murder movies; we've got the ones with good recommendations from friends and reviewers. Can you join with me in asking the Lord to shine the Light on those things? We're in this together. I need you; you need me. The kids need us both. There is dust in our world, but that doesn't mean we have to invite it in and call it our own.

5. Remember you were designed to shine. Maybe the biggest challenge is forgetting what it was like to be shiny and thinking it's normal to be dusty. We aren't quite as dusty as the other guys, so it's okay. We're like the man who visited a psychiatrist complaining, "I've been misbehaving, Doc, and my conscience is troubling me."

The doctor asked, "And you want something that will strengthen your willpower?"

"Well, no," the man replied. "I was thinking of something that would weaken my conscience."

It all goes back to what we are hoping to reproduce in our ministries. If there is dust in our lives, we'll produce dusty disciples. Yet God is famous for cleaning us up and restoring us—making us new all over again. The scrubbing may sting for a moment, but the freedom and joy is well worth the trouble. It's what a life of intimacy with God is all about.

CHAPTER THREE

Living a Life of Honor: The Tough Questions

Several years ago, the new governor of Minnesota shocked me. I was watching him being interviewed on television—this big, outgoing former pro wrestler—right after he was elected. The interviewer asked: "Have you ever been with a prostitute?"

"Yes, I have," the governor answered. The response came without hesitation and seemingly not a shred of shame. "But that was before I got married," he added. At that, the interviewer moved on, completely satisfied, the implication being: *Ah! So you're a "regular kinda guy."*

It seems that society (including many Christians) constantly tries to find ways to maneuver around the question

Moral values that used to be universally accepted are now open for negotiation.

of right or wrong. Moral values that used to be universally accepted are now open for negotiation. In the case of the famous governor, he asserted that it was okay to be with a prostitute, since he was not married. If we were to debate whether this was right or wrong, we could take an eternity—even among ministers—to agree on what is acceptable. Instead of trying to weasel our way through justifying whatever we want to do, why not take the discussion to a higher plane? Instead of asking if it is merely right or wrong, let's ask, "Is it honorable?"

This generation seems to differ from past generations in its view of what it means to live honorably. These days, when the police ask gang members to tell about their bosses or to name their drug suppliers, they think they are living by a standard of honor by saying, "No, I won't rat out my friends." Yet these same people would not hesitate to kill someone they don't even know when told to. This is obviously a skewed sense of honor.

Who topped the charts as the biggest culprit (as far as the media was concerned) during the Clinton scandal several years ago? Linda Tripp. Why? She blew the whistle on the wrongdoing. She was considered a person without honor because she told on a friend.

As Christ-followers, we must have a high standard of honor. And it must rise above justifying the fleshly desires that keep convenient compromises in our lives. As successful Youth Specialists, we must live a step above what the "average" Christian feels okay doing. If we want deep spiritual results, we must be deep spiritual people and live a lifestyle that eradicates worldliness from our lives. So, how do we define honor?

ASK YOURSELF THE HONOR QUESTIONS

Clearly, our culture has a skewed understanding of what's honorable. In the midst of such an environment, how do we discern the honorable path? I believe we can get some help by facing the three tough questions that honor demands of us.

Question #1: Is your heart honorable? An honorable heart will dictate the kinds of relationships you pursue and how you treat people in those relationships. Do you value people as fully worthy human beings?

For example, let's say an associate pastor has been working for two or three years at a certain church. He preaches on occasion in the senior pastor's absence, does counseling, and leads several educational programs. Then one day certain influential people in the congregation say, "You know what, Mr. Associate, I really like it when you preach and teach. You have marvelous gifts; in fact, I like your sermons better than our senior pastor's. If you ever started a church, I would go to your church."

What soon happens to Mr. Associate? He suddenly senses God calling him to start a church! So he follows the

If we want deep spiritual results, we must be deep spiritual people and live a lifestyle that eradicates worldliness from our lives.

Just because a program or plan looks successful doesn't mean it is honorable.

call and launches a church half a mile down the road. "God called me; I can't help it," he says. He opens the doors and has 100 people in the pews, then 200 people, and it keeps growing. "See, it must be the Lord," he says. "Just look how many people are coming."

What has just happened? He has violated a primary principle of honor: *Mr. Associate used another person's "platform" to endear himself to people for his own personal gain.* With honor in our hearts, we cannot use people that way. We can't even say, "But look at all of the people here; it must be God!" Just because a program or plan looks successful doesn't mean it is honorable. If it started with divisiveness, the Holy Spirit is crying out, "Have you no honor?" The bottom line: we should never exploit another person's credibility for our own personal advancement and take something from them.

Consider this scenario. A guest speaker comes from out of town to preach at a church. The people love him and give him a big offering. He comes back into town to preach at *another* church, which loves him and gives him a big offering. This happens with two or three other churches in town. Then, after he's been to town several times, and he knows many people in town who love him, he feels God has called him to start a Bible study . . . in that town.

I'm sure you can see where this is going. He begins an advertising campaign, and all these loving people from the different churches say, "Oh, I am going to go to that Bible study. That's the guy who was such a good preacher!" And so he gets 200 people coming to the Friday night Bible study. Later, of course, God apparently "calls" him to start a church in this town. When he opens the doors, 500 people get sucked out of all the other churches—the same churches that offered him their platform, invited him to preach, and gave him offerings. He has endeared himself to these people and is taking advantage of that for his own benefit. Remember, just because crowds of people followed his lead does not mean he was honorable.

You can see how this same principle would apply to the role of youth pastor. Think again about our example from a previous chapter. You've accepted the role of youth minister and you tell your teens, "I will be here for at least three years." But after one year a "great opportunity from the Lord" comes along and you get a job offer to be a youth pastor on the other side of town and be paid "real money." So you violate your word and accept the job. Yes, you broke trust with all those teens you gave your word to, but they are "out of sight, out of mind." Your teens are now left with the impression that godly leaders lie. Worse still, half of your teens want to come across town to the new youth ministry you are starting. The old church is now divided; you have created a rift with the kids and the congregation.

Living with honor compels us to commit and stay under the blessing of our spiritual leaders. Can you do any of the above and still have honor? Yes, if you have the blessing of your pastor. Yes, if you make it clear that: "We refuse to let anyone who attends the old church come to the new one we are starting." That's harder. But it's honorable.

Never exploit another person's credibility for our own personal advancement.

Living with honor compels us to commit and stay under the blessing of our spiritual leaders.

Question #2: Is your mouth honorable? Having an honorable mouth means that when you say something, you mean it. You don't flippantly "sort of" give your word—"Oh yeah, I'll do that"—and then not follow through.

How many of us have done that? When it suddenly becomes inconvenient to keep a commitment, we look for a way to excuse ourselves from it. But shouldn't we keep our word?

When somebody asks me to pray for them, I say, "Let's pray right now." I don't want to say, "I'll pray for you," and then get busy and forget all about it. I recall a teen who came to me at an Acquire the Fire convention. He asked me to pray for his ailing father. I prayed with him at that moment and then the teen asked whether I was going to continue to pray for his dad.

"I want to, Tim, but I can't promise that for sure," I said. "So that's why I prayed with you right here." I didn't know if I would remember.

The teen asked, "Oh, so are you, like, too important or something?" His voice was full of attitude.

I said, "No, I want to keep my word to you. I may pray for him, but truthfully, I may not because of all the things that I am doing and praying for." Remember that even the smallest promise that comes out of your mouth needs to be kept. Jesus said: "Simply let your 'Yes' be 'Yes,' and your 'No,' 'No'; anything beyond this comes from the evil one"(Matt. 5:37).

Look at this interesting story of deception from the

Book of Joshua. The principle of being honorable with our speech goes all the way back to God's people in the Old Testament:

When the people of Gibeon heard what Joshua had done to Jericho and Ai, they resorted to a ruse: They went as a delegation whose donkeys were loaded with worn-out sacks and old wineskins, cracked and mended. The men put worn and patched sandals on their feet and wore old clothes. All the bread of their food supply was dry and moldy. Then they went to Joshua in the camp at Gilgal and said to him and the men of Israel, "We have come from a distant country; make a treaty with us."

The men of Israel said to the Hivites, "But perhaps you live near us. How then can we make a treaty with you?" . . .

"This bread of ours was warm when we packed it at home on the day we left to come to you. But now see how dry and moldy it is. And these wineskins that we filled were new, but see how cracked they are. And our clothes and sandals are worn out by the very long journey."

The men of Israel sampled their provisions but did not inquire of the Lord. Then Joshua made a treaty of peace with them to let them live, and the leaders of the assembly ratified it by oath.

Three days after they made the treaty with the Gibeonites, the Israelites heard that they were neighbors, living near them. So the Israelites set out and on the third day came to their cities: Gibeon, Kephirah, Beeroth and Kiriath Jearim. But the Israelites did not attack them, because the leaders of the assembly had sworn an oath to them by the Lord, the God of Israel.

The whole assembly grumbled against the leaders, but all the leaders answered, "We have given them our oath by the Lord, the God of Israel, and we cannot touch them now."

—Joshua 9:3–7, 12–19

These leaders suddenly discovered who their neighbors were! Nevertheless, since they had given their word they were compelled to keep it as an act of respect toward God Himself.

Our word means something. Yet how many of us excuse self-serving behavior with the "I heard God's voice anew" excuse. If we used that tactic in the business world, we would get sued—or go to jail!

Being honorable with your mouth is like enlisting in the army. It is your choice beforehand whether or not to join. But once you join, there is no turning back. You cannot get up the next day and say, "Oh, I don't want to go to boot camp," because it's a done deal. Once you give your word, you have no option but to keep it. You are a slave to the word you have given.

One further matter along these lines: don't make the mistake of thinking that it's permissible to go to the person you made the promise to and ask to be released. That unfairly puts the responsibility on the other person; that is, he becomes the bad guy if he *doesn't* release you. That isn't a choice he should have to make. This may soothe your conscience, and you may say that it's better than breaking your word. It isn't, however, the highest standard of honor.

Question #3: Is your mind honorable? Suppose all of your thoughts were splashed on an overhead projector for your church to see on Sunday morning. Are there hidden things you wouldn't want anybody to know? Hear the words of the apostle Paul:

> *Brothers, whatever is true, whatever is noble, whatever is right, whatever is pure, whatever is lovely, whatever is admirable—if anything is excellent or praiseworthy— think about such things.*
>
> —Philippians 4:8

Paul wrote these words because he knew that any of us can look like a saint on the outside and be pretty rotten inside. More serious than that, our thoughts will eventually shape us—one way or another.

To have honor in our thoughts means more than writing down our values on plaques for all to see. We have core values, and we have rules. We are an honorable ministry, but to be honorable people, we must also have pure hearts and minds.

In 2 Corinthians 13:5 we read, "Examine yourselves to see whether you are in the faith; test yourselves. Do you not realize that Christ Jesus is in you—unless, of course, you fail the test?" We preach the Gospel of undiluted grace, yet we must judge ourselves in our progress toward sanctification. It is possible to see where we are in that journey. In fact, it's a moment-by-moment calling.

What, then, is the standard for each of these three levels of honor? I'll be honest with you. There are things that we have done as a ministry in the past that were not honorable. We can't ever be perfect. But as we discover things that are not honorable, we are obligated to make it right with people; we apologize, and we cleanse our hearts. We judge ourselves so that we need not be judged by others. When we discover little bits and pieces of dishonor in our heart, mouth, or head, we can bring these things to the cross and say, "God, I am so sorry. From now on, this is how I will keep my word. This is how I will live with honor."

Suppose all of your thoughts were splashed on an overhead projector for your church to see on Sunday morning.

How easy it is to do the convenient thing, rather than what is right!

DO THE RIGHT THING
(NOT JUST WHAT'S CONVENIENT)

How easy it is to do the convenient thing, rather than what is right! But honor demands that we will choose the long and narrow road that leads to life. Even if there is a quick win or success, and it might be easy, it may not be honorable. We need to grow to the point that we naturally say, "Yes, I could do that, but my honor just won't let me. I could seize that opportunity, or take advantage of that relationship—and no one would even know—but my honor would know, the honor that God has instilled in my heart." The apostle Paul is our honorable exemplar here.

> *Am I not free? Am I not an apostle? Have I not seen Jesus our Lord? Are you not the result of my work in the Lord? Even though I may not be an apostle to others, surely I am to you! For you are the seal of my apostleship in the Lord.*
>
> *This is my defense to those who sit in judgment on me. Don't we have the right to food and drink? Don't we have the right to take a believing wife along with us, as do the other apostles and the Lord's brothers and Cephas? Or is it only I and Barnabas who must work for a living? . . .*
>
> *If others have this right of support from you, shouldn't we have it all the more?*
>
> *But we did not use this right. On the contrary, we put up with anything rather than hinder the gospel of Christ.*
>
> —1 Corinthians 9:1–6, 12

Honor says: "I would rather support myself than cause any misinterpretation of my heart for you in the relationship." In other words, Paul is really saying, "I don't want your money because it might cost too much!" He could have demanded it as anyone else would have done; it was his right. "But I am not involved with you for my personal gain."

Now, as I close this chapter, I must admit that sometimes we do dishonorable things without even realizing it. Let's be on guard here, because we are human, and things can catch us unaware! When we do realize what's happened, we can determine to do something about it immediately.

One fall, while Teen Mania was still based in Tulsa, we had a big fundraising event. We invited teenagers who had been on mission trips to a dinner and encouraged them to bring their parents and supporters. We told everybody about our dream for the coming year and invited the adults to support the ministry of Teen Mania. Later, as that year unfolded, during the regular meetings I had with my senior pastor, I noticed a change in the atmosphere of our relationship. Something began to feel out of place between us, and I didn't know what it was. It just felt colder than it used to be.

"Pastor, is there anything I can do to warm up our relationship?" I finally asked. "It seems like something isn't quite right between us." My words opened the door for him to share with me what he was planning to share quite soon

Choosing the honorable path may (and probably will) require more time, money, and effort, but will invite the favor of God on your life and ministry.

anyway. He related how, the summer before, he had really pushed his congregation of 5,000, saying, "You need to send your kids on missions trips." They took offerings and many kids went on trips.

But then came our fall fundraising event. The pastor had lent his credibility to the idea of kids going on missions, and there we were, saying, "Please come to this fundraising event, even though you've already supported missions, and start helping Teen Mania." To his way of thinking, we were "using" kids who'd been on mission trips in order to raise money for other Teen Mania programs. He said it didn't seem honorable.

I suddenly saw his point. It had seemed like a classic "bait and switch." I sure hadn't planned it that way; it never crossed my mind. But that's how it looked.

I hadn't even realized that what we did was wrong. But as I sat there with egg all over my face, he said, "You know, if I had known about your programming needs, I'd have been happy to help you raise funds. It felt as if you were pulling away something that I gave you for the ministry's sake, the ministry of missions."

I repented, and together we held another fundraiser with the clearest of purposes. He came and told everyone that they really needed to give to this ministry.

Honor means doing what's right even when something else is more convenient and could somehow be justified. It demands that we ask hard questions of ourselves, and it requires us to make restitution in any area where we fail to meet the highest standard. Choosing the honorable path may (and probably will) require more time, money, and effort, but will invite the favor of God on your life and ministry. This is the reward of living with honor.

CHAPTER FOUR

Living a Life of Honor: How You Can Tell

As leaders, we are required to live with honor because we represent the Lord Himself. When most people consider the possible consequences for their sinful actions, their concern is for themselves. As leaders and Youth Specialists, we must consider the consequences to others if we violate our honor. Too many teens have turned their backs on God and walked away because of the horrible compromise they saw in a youth leader. It is our holy obligation to never cause one of these little ones to stumble, to go the extra mile to ensure that we live according to the highest standard of honor.

In this chapter, we'll explore more of the questions that can help us live up to those standards as we grow our ministries.

It is our holy obligation to never cause one of these little ones to stumble, to go the extra mile to ensure that we live according to the highest standard of honor.

CAN GOD TRUST YOU WITH HIS KIDS?

Let's think again about the great Moses as he was leading his "youth group" of weary, thirsty travelers in this recounting from Numbers:

> The Lord said to Moses, "Take the staff, and you and your brother Aaron gather the assembly together. Speak to that rock before their eyes and it will pour out its water. You will bring water out of the rock for the community so they and their livestock can drink."
>
> So Moses took the staff from the Lord's presence, just as he commanded him. He and Aaron gathered the assembly together in front of the rock and Moses said to them, "Listen, you rebels, must we bring you water out of this rock?" Then Moses raised his arm and struck the rock twice with his staff. Water gushed out, and the community and their livestock drank.
>
> But the Lord said to Moses and Aaron, "Because you did not trust in me enough to honor me as holy in the sight of the Israelites, you will not bring this community into the land I give them."
>
> —Numbers 20:7–12

Was God being too hard on Moses? We might think so, until we remember just how spiritually privileged Moses had been. After all, he'd stood before the burning bush, heard God's voice, participated in God's miraculous deliverances, and even received the Commandments directly from God's hands. Moses had been to the holy mountain and come back with his face aglow. Shouldn't someone this close to God share some of His patience and perspective?

You'd think so; but instead he threw a fit in front of everyone who looked to him for godly leadership. He let his flesh have its own way. And God basically said, "Moses, if you are going to lead my people, I can't be wondering when you'll fly off the handle and disrespect Me in front of them. I need to be able to trust you with those you lead."

Can God trust you that way? Does He know you won't let your bad mood destroy His credibility in one reckless action?

The reason we're Youth Specialists is that we want to help kids. The more your ministry is blessed, the more you can help. But the converse is also true: the more influence you have with kids, *the more you can hurt or disillusion them.* That's why living with honor is imperative and not an option. We must keep our flesh under control. Then God can trust us.

Are you holding to an enduring standard? Why is a solid standard so important? Influenced by society's massive confusion over right and wrong, postmodern teens say: "Well, it may be wrong for you, but it isn't really wrong for me. Different things are right for different people." This

The more influence you have with kids, the more you can hurt or disillusion them. That's why living with honor is imperative and not an option.

How ironic that the world paints its lies so beautifully that if we dare reject them as false, our character is called into question: "Come on, why are you so intolerant?"

kind of muddy thinking has seeped into the church from the world's culture, and our young people are saturated with it. We must resist it!

I read something that both shocked and appalled me: Among American adults, only 46 percent think it's wrong to have a baby out of wedlock.[1] We are saturated by media messages in our country and, apparently, if you hear a lie long enough (in full color and with Dolby sound), you start to think it's the truth. How ironic that the world paints its lies so beautifully that if we dare reject them as false, *our character is called into question: "Come on, why are you so intolerant?"*

As leaders who hold to clear and objective moral absolutes, it is imperative that we not only live by those values, but also that we build them into the lives of the teens we influence. We must teach them where truth is found, and how to discern the presence or absence of it in the lives of others. Jesus said, "By their fruit you will recognize them" (Matt. 7:20). We need to see the "fruit" of people's lives and help our teens steer clear when that fruit is poisonous.

Do you avoid even the appearance of evil? We need to shout this Scripture from the mountaintops with our lips and our lives:

> *Each of you should learn to control his own body in a way that is holy and honorable, not in passionate lust*

like the heathen, who do not know God; and that in this matter no one should wrong his brother or take advantage of him. The Lord will punish men for all such sins, as we have already told you and warned you. For God did not call us to be impure, but to live a holy life. Therefore, he who rejects this instruction does not reject man but God, who gives you his Holy Spirit.

—1 Thessalonians 4:4–8

This passage speaks of controlling our bodies in holy and honorable ways. But the principle extends to our approach to morality in general—not just avoiding evil, but avoiding even the *appearance* of evil. "Abstain from all appearance of evil," says 1 Thessalonians 5:22 (KJV). If anything could even be *perceived* as evil, avoid it. If it *looks* wrong, it could scar your honor.

For men, this translates into a simple and unbreakable rule of thumb: *Don't ever be alone with a girl in your youth group.* Don't ever be alone with any female other than your wife. Don't be alone in the car with her, in a room with her—not anywhere. I don't even take our babysitter home. Katie does it, even though she doesn't like having to drive at 11 P.M. It is better than compromising my honor.

Remember this, men: if you're accused, you lose. Case closed. If something doesn't look good, don't do it. Don't give anyone an opportunity to make an assumption that is not true. Do not give any of the youth, their parents, or the church a reason to question your behavior, regardless of how innocent it may be. Living by this principle makes

We need to see the "fruit" of people's lives and help our teens steer clear when that fruit is poisonous.

If something doesn't look good, don't do it.
Don't give anyone an opportunity to make
an assumption that is not true.

things a little bit harder, and a lot less convenient. But that's exactly how it must be in our day.

"But Ron, what about when I travel?" you ask. Here's what I do. When I arrive at the host church or convention site, I make sure I'm with a staff member and never alone. When I arrive at my hotel room, my hosts walk in, inspect it, make sure nobody is in there, then shut the door. If I order room service, I don't even answer the door. My hosts receive the food in their room and bring it over to me. I won't be alone with a woman. I won't enter an elevator with a woman. Guys, we just can't take any chances at all.

A matter of integrity. Benjamin Netanyahu became Israel's prime minister after Yitzhak Rabin was assassinated in 1995. During this crisis, I saw Netanyahu interviewed on television. Because he belonged to the opposing party, he would have run against Rabin in the next election. The news interviewer asked him about this national tragedy. "What do you think this does for you?" the reporter asked. "How will it affect your chances of winning?"

"I can't believe you would ask me that question," Netanyahu replied. "Don't you realize this is about our nation and our dignity? It is not about a party. I refuse to comment on that." I thought to myself, *Now, that is a big man.* Other politicians would have had a self-serving answer to such a question. Netanyahu, however, chose a higher standard of integrity.

Having integrity is a choice. Here are some rules of thumb that will keep you living with honor:

Make integrity an issue before it needs to be. I attended a Billy Graham crusade a few years ago and spoke with one of the staff people who'd been with the organization for 35 years, assisting Rev. Graham. I asked him, "Why does the Billy Graham Association have such an impeccable reputation for integrity?"

"We decided long ago to make integrity an issue when it wasn't an issue," he said. "We wanted to go the extra mile so no one could ever question us, either in the area of finances or morality. The result was that in the '80s, when so many other ministries were financially disintegrating, our organization didn't suffer that way."

They took great pains to make integrity an issue long before they were faced with tough decisions. For years, they intentionally built an ethical foundation, strong enough to withstand any crisis that would come. I encourage you to have ethics and morality in every area of your life. Build a solid foundation now, before the crashing waves hit. Then you will stand in God's strength through it all.

Good intentions don't excuse bad choices. We humans tend to judge ourselves by our intentions and other people by their actions. We think, "Well, I didn't *intend* to do that, so it wasn't really that bad. I didn't *intend* to hurt that person when I broke my word. I didn't *intend* to break my promise, but things changed."

We have armies of politicians in Washington who want us to judge by intention rather than results, by motive rather than consequences. This is a subtle way of avoiding accountability, something that's crucial to Christian fellowship and effective Christian leadership. We can't sink to that level in youth ministry.

Having integrity is a choice.

I encourage you to have ethics and morality in every area of your life. Build a solid foundation now, before the crashing waves hit. Then you will stand in God's strength through it all.

Always be "working on something" right now. The way to raise your standard of honor is to continuously work on developing your character. This doesn't mean that you can lift yourself up by your bootstraps or whip yourself into shape on your own. Rather, to "develop your character" means to open your heart for Christ's work in you. Consciously, daily, invite Him to transform your thoughts and deeds.

> *Do not conform any longer to the pattern of this world, but be transformed by the renewing of your mind. Then you will be able to test and approve what God's will is— his good, pleasing and perfect will.*
>
> —Romans 12:2

So, what are you working on right now? What part of your honor or your character are you asking Christ to renew? Here are some of the issues that developing Youth Specialists must work on:

How do you treat your senior pastor? It's easy to support him when you both agree. But when you disagree with an authority or pastor, how do you respond? What do you say and do? A run-of-the-mill youth leader might put down his senior pastor all the time (but a Youth Specialist would never find this acceptable). That is totally dishonorable.

Work on it! Pray for him and never say one word—not even an innuendo or gesture—that would imply disrespect.

How quickly do you shut down improper communication? If somebody starts to tell a joke, and you can see that it's going south, what do you do? Do you say, "Don't tell me the punch line"? That would take some self-control, right? And suppose somebody starts telling you some "interesting information" about a brother in Christ? Can you say, "Stop, I don't want to hear it"? The problem is, people are much more willing to say dishonorable things than we are willing to stop them. We can work on it, though.

How do you treat your spouse and children in front of others? What kinds of comments do people hear you making about your spouse? What about your kids? How do you treat your kids? I was probably a pretty challenging kid, but I can remember a time when friends of the family came over to the house, and I overheard my mother telling them how bad we kids were. I was cut to the core and lived with low self-esteem for a long time afterward. After I began to grow in the Lord, I realized she wasn't really describing how bad we were as much as she was expressing her frustration at not being able to figure out how to get us to obey. There's a difference. It was her problem. Remember, when people speak negatively about somebody else, they are speaking negatively about themselves.

How well do you handle personal praise? You'll be tested in this area, because you will receive praise, and it

The way to raise your standard of honor is to continuously work on developing your character.

What kinds of comments do people hear you making about your spouse? What about your kids? How do you treat your kids?.

will grow pretty quickly. I promise you this. You will be rocking the place and reaching kids. It will be exciting, and you will have to guard against pride because everyone will be telling you how great you are. Don't start believing this lie, because God is the great one, not you. Not me. We must take ourselves out of the picture and give God the glory.

So I leave you with this: the best way to stay humble is to stay real before God, realizing who He is and who you are. If you are having break-loose quiet times with God every day and really aggressively seeking Him, you will peel off flesh daily. It is impossible to have a prideful, haughty attitude if you are really in the presence of God every day. It reminds you that He is God, and you are not. This keeps us all humble and seeking to live with *honor*.

1. H.B. London, "Society's Moral Boundaries Sway," taken from Gallup's annual Values and Beliefs survey, May 20, 2005, http://216.109.125.130/search/cach?p=%22Christians%22baby+out+of+wedlock%22+Barna&prssweb=Search&ei=UTF-8&fl=www.family.org/pastor/pwbe/print/pwbe (accessed October 25, 2005).

CHAPTER FIVE

Mandate for the Family: Man in Ministry

I had come to a marital fork in the road. The road happened to be in India. It was hot, I was deathly tired, and my lips still burned from a less-than-satisfying meal of red-hot curry chicken. The worst part: Katie wanted to go home. *Day Two of a six-week preaching tour, and Katie wants to leave?*

We'd set up speaking engagements all over the country; Hindu people were waiting to hear the Gospel. I was pumped (even with my curry-burned lips). Our faces appeared on posters in a number of little villages, proclaiming in all the various dialects: "Come and see Ron and Katie Luce, evangelists from America!" (They thought we were big shots; they didn't know it was just us.) We had arrived in the country at 4 A.M.

after an all-night flight. The folks who picked us up at the airport had smiled and asked, "Are you feeling fresh?"

Are you kidding? Our heads were pounding!

After a few hours of sleep, we enjoyed a sweltering, four-hour train ride, standing shoulder to shoulder with people for much of the ride. We arrived at a missionary bungalow that was just a little more "elegant" than the excrement-daubed huts surrounding it . . . and don't even ask about the bugs!

By this time, my lips weren't hurting quite as much. But Katie was hurting. "Ron, this is just too hard," she said. "Why don't you go on without me? I can head back to Bombay and stay there with some missionaries until you're through."

That's where I hit the crossroads, one of those pivotal places in my life. Have you been there? *Am I going to choose ministry over my spouse?* That was the core of the decision.

I knew that whatever I did here, Katie would remember it for the rest of our lives. I felt the call of the hurting masses, and I felt the call of a yearning spouse, to whom I had committed my whole life. I knew that people were expecting us to appear all over the country for the next six weeks. This was a young preacher's dream; yet somehow, I knew I'd better make the right call here, or this would be the first of many "bad calls." I told Katie I would not go on without her. I would go back to Bombay with her. I told her whatever she wanted to do, I would do it, but . . .

"Before you tell me what you want to do, think about this. For centuries, the reason India has been so desperate for the Gospel is that the devil has used the primitive, difficult circumstances to chase missionaries away. It seems too hard. That is why there are over a billion without the Gospel in India today. Are we going to let the devil chase us off too? I know it's hard, Katie," I said, "but I can't do it without you. I won't."

Something on the inside of Katie just rose up. "We

won't let the devil run us off!" she said, with firm determination in her voice. We prayed. We covenanted together. And we went together, traveling all over that land, sweating in trains, living in huts, and yes, burning our mouths on foreign spices. And Katie saw even more miracles than I did.

YOUR MARRIAGE: THE FIRST PRIORITY

Do you realize that having a world-class family and having a world-class youth ministry are not mutually exclusive? You don't have to have one at the expense of the other. Yet I hear story after story of ministers' families falling apart, of pastors who threw themselves into ministry at the expense of their families.

How can we make sure this doesn't happen to us? I believe the answer lies in keeping our marriages strong, healthy, and based upon biblical principles. A key passage is Ephesians 5:21–33. Look closely at Paul's words:

> *Submit to one another out of reverence for Christ.*
>
> *Wives, submit to your husbands as to the Lord. For the husband is the head of the wife as Christ is the head of the church, his body, of which he is the Savior. Now as the church submits to Christ, so also wives should submit to their husbands in everything.*
>
> *Husbands, love your wives, just as Christ loved the church and gave himself up for her to make her holy, cleansing her by the washing with water through the word, and to present her to himself as a radiant church, without stain or wrinkle or any other blemish, but holy and blameless. In this same way, husbands ought to love their wives as their own bodies. He who loves his wife loves himself. After all, no one ever hated his own body, but he feeds and cares for it, just as Christ does the church—for we are members of his body. "For this*

reason a man will leave his father and mother and be united to his wife, and the two will become one flesh." This is a profound mystery—but I am talking about Christ and the church. However, each one of you also must love his wife as he loves himself, and the wife must respect her husband.

—Ephesians 5:21–33

Many marriages in ministry don't *end up* being very wholesome because they weren't wholesome *to begin with.* Sure, these folks had a heart for kids, so they got involved in ministry; but when their marriages hit hard times, they blamed the ministry. The truth is, they really shouldn't have been in ministry until they had developed an enduring, healthy marriage. Wholesome marriage is all about our priorities, so let's dig into six principles for keeping our marriages a first-class priority.

Pray over your marriage with godly vision. I do this almost every day. I pray not just for my wife but for the kind of marriage we have—and will have in the future. *God, be in the midst of this relationship with us!*

Together, we've determined we'll have a marriage that's strong in the Lord. We won't settle for barely hanging on just because we have a marriage license. We'll deeply love one another—and love being with one another.

We actually put together a Marriage Mission Statement soon after our wedding. We put our ideas together, everything we'd learned about marriage by reading books and receiving the wise counsel of marriage veterans. We asked ourselves, over several weeks: "What do we want our marriage to be?" Then we composed a detailed statement, about three paragraphs long, which Katie wrote in calligraphy. We put some artwork around it and framed it.

Now there's no doubt in our minds what our marriage stands for. When we pray over our relationship, we include the kinds of things appearing in that beautiful vision on the wall. We had to take the time and effort, though, to soberly discern: "What, really, do we want as the fruit of this marriage?"

Together, read the best books about marriage. Over the years, we've read some great books about marriage. We discuss them, share what points made impact, and consider how we might apply the new information. The point is, in any marriage there are things we should be talking about with our spouses. But how do we know what those things are? And who will remind us?

Books can come to the rescue here. After all, any relationship can grow a bit dull if the persons involved always talk about the same old things: How was your day? How are the kids? What's for dinner? (That last one is a favorite of mine . . . unless it's curry chicken.)

Reading together and talking about the qualities of a good marriage bring fresh insight to the relationship. I would encourage you to do this on a regular basis. And, gentlemen, did you know that when you bring the book home, your wife feels a deeper sense of security: *He cares about this marriage; he wants us to grow and develop together.* You can develop your ministry and build your marriage as well.

What books are good to read? Here are just a few we've enjoyed:

Fit to Be Tied, by Lynne and Bill Hybels
For Better or for Best, by Gary and Norma Smalley
The Five Love Languages, by Gary Chapman
Communication: Key to Your Marriage, by H. Norman
    Wright
Men and Women: The Giving of Self, by Larry Crabb

You are one flesh, not one spirit. You never become one spirit. You become one in spirit.

Submit to one another as brother and sister in Christ. This principle flows directly from Paul's words to the Ephesians above. Men typically go right to verse 22 and notice that wives are supposed to submit to their husbands as to the Lord. And, of course, it's an all-time favorite passage of Scripture . . . for husbands. (Many husbands who aren't even Christians know this one.)

Some Christian husbands use this Scripture as permission to force their wives to bend to their will. Somehow they miss the statement in verse 21 where God calls the husband and wife to submit to one another.

You see, before you were married you were brother and sister in the Lord. And you still are, though you're now more than that. Your *unity* in the Spirit is the same as that existing between you and every other believer, but your *union* is of the flesh. Do you see the distinction? You are one flesh, not one spirit. You never become one spirit. You become *one in spirit* when you believe and receive the indwelling Holy Spirit. You don't *become* one spirit when you get married; you should *be* united by one Spirit before you are married, as two believers.

God expects brothers and sisters in the church to respect each other and listen to each other, to honor each other in every way. Here in Ephesians 5:21, we're called to mutually submit to one another, just as all believers must do among themselves. This means that I don't always have to be right. I may be the male, but that doesn't mean I am always right. I'm a human being and very fallible.

Then comes the specific application of this submission: wives are to submit to their husbands as they submit to the Lord, and men are to love their wives more than they love their own bodies. Which is the more "submissive" stance, then?

Clearly, if both partners are submitting to Christ and loving as He loves them, they will show the deepest regard for one another. No trampling. No refusing to listen. No plowing ahead without due consultation.

Here's how it works for us. Katie and I promised from the beginning of our marriage that we would never do anything unless we were in full agreement. Sometimes she really wants to do one thing, and I really want to do another. What do we do? We just wait. We say, "We'll eventually get some insight about this, and we'll figure out the right thing to do." We wait before the Lord.

I've always thought it's best to be in full agreement on what we do, even if that means we do fewer things. That way, I know my wife is with me, heart and soul, and that every decision we make contributes to our togetherness. The result? I've learned to trust my spouse. I've also come to realize that I'm not the only one who can hear from God.

Gentlemen, do you know what headship means? Review again what Paul writes:

> *The husband is the head of the wife as Christ is the head of the church, his body, of which he is the Savior. Now as*

Wholesome marriage is all about our priorities, so let's . . . keep our marriages a first-class priority.

I've learned to trust my spouse. I've also come to realize that I'm not the only one who can hear from God.

> *the church submits to Christ, so also wives should submit to their husbands in everything.*
>   —Ephesians 5:23–24

Being the head does not mean that we get our way every time. Be the head, *not* the dictator, as Christ is the head of the church. Ephesians tells us that spouses are to mutually submit to each other, but sometimes a decision *must* be made and we just can't come to agreement. At those times, the husband must humbly submit to his headship calling and make the decision. Husbands, it's not a matter of wielding authority; it's more like sticking your neck out and saying, "I sure hope I'm hearing from God on this!"

Katie and I have been married for decades, and we haven't needed to take this path more than five times. With almost all of our decisions, we either agree or we wait. Those few times when I've exercised headship decision-making, I've sensed an anointing, a leading that comes from God. Many times a right decision can be made without us even understanding *why*. It is a matter of humble, reverent trust in God. It's far from a spiritualized "power play."

Men, we need to give our wives the confidence that, when necessary, their husbands will have the headship anointing to lead in a particular, tough decision-making circumstance. Then they can say, "Even if I don't understand the decision, I will trust God."

But husbands, I would caution not to take advantage of headship. True headship is neither dominating nor dictating. It is trusting and listening. It's a "we thing," not a "me thing."

Keep a healthy friendship intact. Someone once said, "Marriages are made in heaven, but people are responsible for the maintenance." I agree! A wedding isn't a marriage. A wedding is just the beginning; then the work begins.

But it can be joyful work. For one thing, our spouses aren't just marriage partners, they're our best friends too. Scripture gives us many principles related to healthy friendship that we can draw upon in our marital relationships.

Consider John 15:15, for example: *"I no longer call you servants, because a servant does not know his master's business. Instead, I have called you friends, for everything that I learned from my Father I have made known to you."* Wow! Jesus, Friend, shares His heart with us. Can you share your heart with your mate?

Ephesians 4:29 gives us more great relational help: *"Do not let any unwholesome talk come out of your mouths, but only what is helpful for building others up according to their needs, that it may benefit those who listen."* How many people speak unwholesomely about their spouses? If there's an issue, shouldn't we talk it out, "speaking the truth in love" (vs. 15)? Furthermore, according to 4:31–32, we must: *"Get rid of all bitterness, rage and anger, brawling and slander, along with*

True headship is neither dominating nor dictating. It is trusting and listening. It's a "we thing," not a "me thing."

A wedding isn't a marriage. A wedding is just the beginning; then the work begins.

every form of malice. Be kind and compassionate to one another, forgiving each other, just as in Christ God forgave you." Wise counsel for any marriage.

But the most practical action, which can virtually guarantee our growth in all of these principles, comes in Ephesians 4 verse 26: *"Do not let the sun go down while you are still angry."* Any time humans interact, conflict may enter the relationship, but that doesn't mean we have to leave it there. We are intelligent beings; we can talk things out. As angry as we may legitimately be, we can refuse to let that anger draw us into sin. And we can make sure we go to bed with peace in our hearts about our love for one another, whether or not we've been able to resolve a particular problem.

As we approach our weddings, most of us consider the event as if it means entering into a settled state of life, as if we're joining a club. Once it's done, our membership is set. But suppose we changed the analogy a bit? Suppose we saw the wedding as embarking on a journey or entering a course of instruction that will last for a lifetime? We have the great privilege of spending life's years with our lover, learning to become the best of friends. What could be better?

Set up a 777 Plan—and stick to it! This is one of the things Katie and I do, no matter how busy we are. What is the 777 Plan? Every seven days we have family day, every seven weeks we have a three-day get away, and every seven months we have some kind of vacation or one-week excursion (either just Katie and me or with the kids).

Ministers are often the busiest people of all. Why? We hear the cries of others; we're moved to reach them, touch them, and help them with all the resources of God's goodness and grace. In the midst of this awesome motivation, we can leave our families in the dust. In fact, I think one of the biggest fears of wives is that their minister husbands will leave them lonely. "Will I even know you, once our kids are grown?" they wonder.

The 777 Plan can help protect us here. It's simple, and if you promise to stand by it, the whole family will know: regardless of your busy schedule, when those "sevens" come around, you are back together having family fun. Using the plan doesn't mean we don't talk and relate at other times. It simply means that we choose to focus on these times as the bare minimum, written in stone.

It's a matter of applying discipline to our personal schedules. Amazingly, in talking with others in ministry or business who never leave town, I find I'm spending more family time than they are! So, have a plan, and stick to the plan.

FAMILY AND MINISTRY: THEY GO TOGETHER

I began this chapter by stressing that you can have a great family and have a great ministry too. Then we moved on to explore the foundational principle underneath: put the love of your spouse above the love of your work. If this means shutting down and walking away from ministry for a while to make sure your marriage stays strong, then do it.

Moving on in Ephesians 5, we hear the apostle saying, "cleansing her by the washing with water through the word, and to present her to himself as a radiant church, without stain or wrinkle or any other blemish, but holy and blameless" (vss. 26–27). One of the ways to love your wife is to build her up. Washing her with the word means helping her to grow in the Lord. It's not that she can't do things for herself, but she knows that *you care about her spiritual nutrition.*

Someone has said that the best thing you can do for your kids is to love your wife. It's true!

She knows you're interested in that part of her and not that she's just fending for herself.

All of this involves the whole family, of course, including the kids. Remember our Marriage Mission Statement? We did something similar for our family relationships; we developed a written Family Covenant with the kids. We came up with four main points of character that we want our family to stand for. We talked with the kids about where (in the Scripture) those qualities came from, and then Katie wrote it up in calligraphy on parchment paper. Yes, another nice frame for the wall!

We made a big ceremony of this, announcing the event days in advance. I broke a brick in half and showed that the stuff inside the brick makes it strong. "Just like that," I told the kids, "the stuff inside our family makes us strong—or not." Then we talked about all four of the character traits we want inside our family. "Can we work really hard to make sure this is a part of our heart and the way our family lives?"

Each person had his or her comments about the covenant, and then we prayed over the document before each of us signed it. Finally, we made little laminated cards for each member, listing the four character traits of the Luce family. A couple of the kids made necklaces out of them.

Covenants are good, but someone has said that the best thing you can do for your kids is to love your wife. It's true! And I would add: be a "governing unit" with her. Let your kids see your deep affection for her, and always be a solid front with her in disciplinary matters. Beyond this, I invite you to pay attention to a few practical DOs and DON'Ts.

DO *really listen to your kids.* I put this first, because everything else hinges on it. If kids know you're listening, they can overcome virtually any other problem that may arise between the two of you. Patient, active listening shows a caring, loving heart. And love conquers all.

There comes a point in a child's developmental process, too, when they begin listening for *you*. They want you to say something coherent back to them after you've listened. At that point I realized it wasn't enough for me to just go through the motions and physically be in the same room. *I had to tune into them.* I had to connect with them. How else could I know what was really going on within them?

These days we hear a lot about teens making bombs in their basements or going to school with machine guns. I can't explain it, but I'm quite sure the parents were disconnected from these kids. We can't let that happen! I encourage you to listen when the windows into their hearts are wide open. Be there; hear them; respond. The standard pattern is for a teen to say something like, "Sometimes I just feel really lonely"—and then they just kind of stop. They are waiting to see whether you are an open vessel for them. Are you ready to receive what's next? A window is opening, if you really begin to listen. Seize those moments. All you need to do is be quiet, or reflect back the feeling in the simplest way—"Lonely, huh?" Then the conversation continues.

DON'T *let just "any old thing" into your house.* "I will set before my eyes no vile thing," says Psalm 101:3. I would

Put the love of your spouse above the love of your work.

Why keep all the ministry to yourself? Involve your kids, even on mission trips.

extend it like this: "I will let no vile thing come before the eyes of my family." We can frame all the family documents we want, but if the world is bombarding our kids at will every day, how can we fight back?

First, put a filter on your Internet. Don't rely on software filters, because teens can often find ways to "hack" them. Instead, sign up with an Internet service provider that filters content at the server level. There are scores of such companies to choose from, but you might start your search with Web sites like these . . .

- www.afafilter.com
- www.hedge.org
- www.cnonline.net
- christianbroadband.com

Second, why not unplug the television set? We unplugged ours and just watch videos instead. Yes, we can hook the television back up for special things like a ball game, now and then, but we rarely do it. I trust my kids, but I don't trust that crazy Hollywood. (There are a lot of benefits; it's amazing how many toys my kids *don't* ask for anymore.)

DO involve them in the ministry. Why keep all the ministry to yourself? Involve your kids, even on mission trips. I'm getting ready to leave with them for Mexico in a couple of weeks. I'm taking the girls one week, and my son the next. I ask the kids to bring some of their toys that they'd like to give away to the children of the world. As they're giving, I arrange for a translator, so the kids can tell about Jesus at the same time.

See how it works? Whatever your ministry, get them involved. If God has called you, then He has called you as a family.

DON'T fear "touchy-feely" relating. Men, hug your kids and express emotion with them, whether they are boys or girls. My experiences at Acquire the Fire events give me this principle. Quite often I end up praying with and for kids who are deeply wounded by family situations. I have seen thousands of gallons of tears cried at altars all across America. *Most of these young people have not been hugged by their dads.*

A girl came to a concert one summer and then wrote me a note afterward, asking to go on a mission trip. She said, "The reason is because when I met you in that crowd, you hugged me. When I felt that hug, I felt like God was hugging me." But the effect of a hug from Dad goes far beyond that. Let's not be "too big a man" to hug. If your daughter doesn't get a hug from you, she will go to get a hug from a guy, maybe an ungodly kind of hug. One way or the other, she'll long for the manly affection that Dad never gave her.

I have learned a couple of things along the way, especially when it comes to daughters. My daughters and I have a secret handshake. We can be holding hands at any

If kids know you're listening, they can overcome virtually any other problem that may arise between the two of you.

When kids see a little bit of humility in their dads, it goes a long way.

time and we don't have to say a thing to communicate our love. We will do four squeezes. I'll do four squeezes first, maybe, and it stands for "Do you love me?" Then she will do three, "Yes, I do." Then I do two, "How much?" And then she'll just squeeze and keep holding. Or maybe she will start it. It's our secret; we look at each other, and we know what's going on.

Do be ready to ask their forgiveness. I've had to do it myself, quite often. It works wonders.

Last night I was cooking dinner, and Hannah was helping me. She was grating some cheese next to a cup of garlic I had just sliced. She went to take a bite of the cheese and grabbed a piece of the garlic by mistake. Immediately, she began spitting it out all over the cheese!

"Hannah! What are you doing," I snapped at her. "Do you realize you have a cold? Leave the kitchen, now! . . . Well, you can stay; just don't *help* me."

I could tell I'd wounded her heart. I repented and apologized. I looked at her and said, "I don't care if I have to throw this all away and start over again. I should never treat you like that. I'm sorry." When kids see a little bit of humility in their dads, it goes a long way.

Don't just endure. Some men approach all of this thinking, "Okay, I have to add my family to my list." As if they just have to endure another added task! They figure, "Well, I do put food on the table and a roof over their heads, so I am a good father. Do I really owe more?"

But being a father *is* more. It's imparting life, character, love, and the love of God to our kids. Would you commit to being that kind of man?

It's time for us to prioritize, if we want to have a world-class family and ministry. You don't have to have a great ministry and a lame family. You can have both. However, you must count the cost and pay the price.

Having a great family takes concerted effort, it will not come automatically. Remember: nobody ever had a baby and hoped that it would get hooked on drugs one day. Nobody ever walked down the aisle and hoped they would end up with a nice divorce. They all had great intentions, but did not act on their desires. We all want great things, but we only get results by paying the price of heartfelt commitment, leaning on the grace of God for every accomplishment.

Having a family is a sacrifice. You either sacrifice up front, or you will sacrifice the rest of your life. If you don't sacrifice while they are young, then for the next 20, 30, 40 years (they are older a lot longer than they are younger) you may be paying the price of your kids having babies out of wedlock, going through divorces, and walking away from

REACHING HER CLASSMATES

It all started with my 13-year-old daughter and I praying about reaching her classmates and then her school. Within five months, every classmate was coming to our service, and some gave their lives to Christ!

—Glenn, Youth Specialist

If you sacrifice now, love them and pour your time into them, you will reap the benefit for the rest of your life.

the Lord. If you sacrifice now, love them and pour your time into them, you will reap the benefit for the rest of your life.

I like what one famous preacher told me, "I promised God I am taking four people to heaven with me. My wife and three children are going with me for sure, and everyone else I bring is frosting on the cake."

Let us all have the courage to keep our family and ministry in proper order.

CHAPTER SIX

God's Call for the Family Woman

(This chapter is a little different. Let me introduce Katie, my amazing wife. She'll be speaking to you here, directing her comments to our women readers, particularly the wives of men in ministry. But that doesn't mean you husbands can skip this chapter. It's absolutely crucial that you understand where the ladies are coming from as you work at having a great ministry and a wonderful family life together. So listen up!]

Ladies, I'd like you to imagine us talking together over coffee some afternoon. If I had a chance to sit down with you, and we had a long conversation, I'm sure we could learn a lot from one another. But since this is a book chapter, I'm going to

Join in your husband's vision. It is a serious thing when the wife stands aloof in her heart from the vision of her husband.

have to do all the talking! Still, if we were to chat, what would you remember from our conversation? I'm going to guess that a few statements like the following would stick in your mind . . .

"Watch out for the pearls!" I want you to hear how important this is: join in your husband's vision. It is a serious thing when the wife stands aloof in her heart from the vision of her husband. He may withdraw his own heart and ministry from you without even intending to do so. Jesus taught this principle:

> *Give not that which is holy unto the dogs, neither cast ye your pearls before swine, lest they trample them under their feet, and turn again and rend you.*
> —Matthew 7:6 (KJV)

There was a time when I was acting the part of the "swine" with my husband. Yet he graciously persisted in laying the pearls of his vision for ministry before me and inviting me to enter it with him.

When we first started Teen Mania, my heart wasn't in it at all; I was completely focused on foreign missions. You see, we had traveled overseas for six months, and we both had missions on our hearts. I felt sure that our life's calling would have something to do with missions. I knew that I was called to full-time ministry, but Ron and I weren't exactly sure what the Lord had planned for us. During this time we traveled to 25 different countries and saw God move in powerful, mind-blowing ways.

We prepared our hearts before we went, praying that we would lay hands on the sick for healing and that people would come to know the Lord in droves. And it happened. In India, we saw two ladies healed of blindness; as I prayed I watched their eyes turn from cloudy white back to beautiful brown. I also saw a lady get up and walk—someone who hadn't walked in years and years! Best of all, over 20 thousand people came to know the Lord as a result of just the two of us preaching the Gospel. We saw Hindus wiping the dots off their foreheads, pulling off the bracelets symbolizing their worship of a myriad of other gods.

Now, if you were me—if you'd seen all these things happen before your eyes—would you be excited about missions? I was overwhelmed; I was sure this was our calling. However, while we were in Indonesia, we fasted for three days, laying our lives before the Lord and asking Him specifically what we were to do. I was praying, with missions on my heart; Ron was praying, with missions on his heart.

But the Lord had put teenagers on his heart too.

American teenagers.

So he shared that with me—cast his pearls before me. And I said, "You have got to be crazy!"

"But Katie . . ."

"Ron, think about all we've seen. Then think about those American teenagers—they have a church on every street corner. Where is the need here?"

"But Katie . . ."

"Those kids can turn on the radio and get saved—but look at these people. They've never heard the name of Jesus before. Are you *crazy*?"

Ron was gracious. "Let's just pray about it," he said.

So we went home, and I began to pray about it like this: "Lord, if You have really put this on his heart, then stir up my heart too, because I don't have one ounce of burden for teenagers. I am intimidated by them, and I don't know how to relate to them anymore."

That's when the Lord opened up my eyes and showed me the big picture. (I need to see the big picture to know *why* we're doing what were doing. Are you like that?) I began to *see* teenagers in a new and fearful light—how the evil one had ravaged them with gangs and drugs, suicide and sex. I saw a whole generation with broken hearts, and then I saw God and *His* heart for these young people. It seemed the Lord Himself was ready to raise up the standard of youth ministry.

I also saw that, in those days, there were barely any youth pastors being paid a salary. Youth ministry wasn't a priority to very many pastors or to the church body at large. But I saw what God wanted to do and I became so excited about it. I began to see the vision, how we could take teenagers—this broken generation—and help them know God's plan for their lives. God could be glorified through their changed lives. Then I thought about this: how many of these thousands and thousands of teens calling out for help *might someday travel to the mission field and far outstrip anything Ron and I had ever done there?*

Of course, that is exactly what God has been doing over the years since my own heart was broken for teens. Through Teen Mania, countless young people have gone overseas to pray for the sick, minister in the name of Jesus, and witness the victory of the cross over illness and death. Year after year God has multiplied our efforts beyond our greatest imagination, and He is glorified.

All of this to say, *share the ministry vision with your husband.* God knew what He was doing when He put the two of you together. You are one with him; you are called together with him. He put that vision in your husband, and

He will put it in you. But also pay attention to the pearls of God's vision, the priceless treasure of doing His will as a family.

"You're either building or destroying the ministry." You may have a Mr. Gung-Ho Preacher husband filled with awesome vision, and sometimes it feels like you're being carried along by his momentum. But it matters just as much where *your* heart is in the ministry. I remember the days when I had real little ones at home, two- and three-year olds, and I just rode along on Ron's coattails. I figured, "Why do I need to get up early and pray? I'm changing diapers all the time, and who needs to be anointed for that? Ron is the one out there speaking and counseling, so why do I need to be anointed?" That is a lie from the pit. *You have the power to make or break your ministry as a couple.*

> *The wise woman builds her house, but with her own hands the foolish one tears hers down.*
> —Proverbs 14:1

God must think we are pretty important to give us that kind of power in our homes. And be assured, this has everything to do with ministry, for a ministry rests on the pillars of family unity. It flows from the wholeness of the couple together, from the quality of their walk with God together. That is, the health of your family unit determines the health of your ministry. And the enemy has taken the offensive (if

Share the ministry vision with your husband. God knew what He was doing when He put the two of you together.

You have the power to make or break your ministry as a couple.

you haven't already noticed!) to destroy homes because of this truth. He knows that if he can tear down families, he can devastate the effectiveness of the church. So let us be wise to his schemes!

Ron and I were driving to the airport one day, along with two church leaders who were shepherding a church in trouble. In fact, their church was falling apart before their eyes. As we talked, my heart grieved for these men. The senior pastor's wife had left him to pursue her own career. You see, her husband was very zealous for the Lord—so zealous that he had neglected his home life. The associate pastor seemed to be in the same boat. They were hard workers, but their families were in shambles, and their church was no better.

As we talked with these two men, we realized that they were broken, confused, and deeply wounded. This was the leadership of the church! They weren't wimpy little guys— they were strong in the Lord—yet because of their two messed-up families, a whole body of believers suffered and withered on the vine. How important it is to manage our homes wisely and well! It's a two-person job.

He must manage his own family well and see that his children obey him with proper respect.
—1 Timothy 3:4

Even in laying out the requirements for church leadership, God put the priority on family and its management. He cares so much that we are strong and united in Him and His work. In youth ministry this has special importance because, day in and day out, you minister to teenagers who face serious family dysfunction—or no family structure at all. So when you come to them with a strong marriage and family, you speak powerfully into their lives before you even open your mouth.

You and your husband are like the head and the heart of your family. If the head and the heart break down, then the whole body dies. Similarly, together you are the head and the heart of your youth ministry.

Make your husband your priority, and don't get sidetracked by placing your children at the center of everything. Love your children with all your heart, more than your own life, but never let them run the home. Sadly, it is all too easy to make your home an exclusively child-centered environment. This is especially true when you have new babies with all their legitimate demands, day and night. You give them every ounce of your being, all your energy and love. What a challenge, then, to keep that priority of loving your husband first!

But this is your calling. This is the path to loving your child in the deepest way—to stay "one" with your husband. Only then will the family be all that your child needs it to be. You are to make your husband the priority because your children are counting on that from the bottom of their hearts. Whether they can express it verbally or not, it is exactly what they need. Your rock-solid relationship with your husband is their refuge, their whole security in life.

A ministry rests on the pillars of family unity. It flows from the wholeness of the couple together, from the quality of their walk with God together.

Make your husband your priority, and don't get sidetracked by placing your children at the center of everything.

"If you don't let him go, you'll lose him." Here is a Scripture I love to pray over my husband:

> *The king's heart is in the hand of the Lord; he directs it like a watercourse wherever he pleases.*
> —Proverbs 21:1

I believe with all my heart that God is directing Ron's heart. He is the "king" in our family, so I pray this verse over him. Clearly, there is, for me, an aspect of letting go in this verse: letting go of my own husband and trusting his heart into the hand of the Lord.

I am a living testimony to the power of holding on. I was terrified of letting my husband go. Why? Because my husband is such a "go-getter." He's a visionary; as God directs, he will follow.

When we got married, Ron would say things like, "I have to go. I have to travel. We can't influence the kind of people that God wants us to influence if we just stay right here in peace and comfort." Every time he would say those things, I'd feel a big lump form in my throat. I'd grit my teeth and fight to hold back the fear. Where was my security? I wanted to scream, "No! Just stay here with me!"

A certain Scripture helped me at this point, though:

> *David, wearing a linen ephod, danced before the LORD with all his might, while he and the entire house of Israel*

brought up the ark of the LORD with shouts and the sound of trumpets.

As the ark of the LORD was entering the City of David, Michal daughter of Saul watched from a window. And when she saw King David leaping and dancing before the LORD, she despised him in her heart.

They brought the ark of the LORD and set it in its place inside the tent that David had pitched for it, and David sacrificed burnt offerings and fellowship offerings before the LORD. After he had finished sacrificing the burnt offerings and fellowship offerings, he blessed the people in the name of the LORD Almighty. Then he gave a loaf of bread, a cake of dates and a cake of raisins to each person in the whole crowd of Israelites, both men and women. And all the people went to their homes.

When David returned home to bless his household, Michal daughter of Saul came out to meet him and said, "How the king of Israel has distinguished himself today, disrobing in the sight of the slave girls of his servants as any vulgar fellow would!"

David said to Michal, "It was before the LORD, who chose me rather than your father or anyone from his house when he appointed me ruler over the LORD's people Israel—I will celebrate before the LORD. I will become even more undignified than this, and I will be humiliated in my own eyes. But by these slave girls you spoke of, I will be held in honor."

And Michal daughter of Saul had no children to the day of her death.

—2 Samuel 6:14–23

Apparently King David was a go-getter too. He danced so enthusiastically before the Lord that his clothes fell off! And his wife despised him for it.

She wasn't blessed for that attitude, but she instructs me. I have always prayed, "Lord, don't ever let me get between Ron and You, what You want to do in his life and in our life together. Don't ever let me despise Your work in him!"

During the first year of my marriage, I called home to Mom, thoroughly frustrated. Ron's heart was "out there with God," as usual. He happened to be away from home, and I felt as if his heart was so involved with the ministry that nothing was left for me. I told my Mom these things. But did she encourage my complaints? No. She simply raised the question: "Katie, can you thank God that Ron is out doing God's work?" God began to deal with me, and I began to let Ron go.

Then the message was reinforced when I received a letter from a good friend who lives in Panama. She's a missionary there with her husband, raising their children in the jungle. She is an incredible woman with great wisdom, whom I deeply respect. "I had to let my husband go," she said. "I had to die to that grasping, that longing for a security based in my husband. How else could I learn to rest in the security of God?"

Sometimes her husband would need to go deep into the jungle to find new tribes who'd never heard of Jesus. He couldn't know in advance what he'd find, whether the people would be friendly or deadly hostile. He would be gone for days, sometimes weeks at a time, with no ability to communicate back with her. She had to let him go because God was directing him and her in the work. "If you do not let your husband go like that, Katie," she wrote, "then you will lose him. It's a scary, blessed paradox, isn't it?"

She told me that God put the "go" in our husbands' hearts, and so we must let them do all that God has called them to do. So with the fear of God in my heart, I did let Ron go. And God has been faithful to me in all of the things that I desire for our marriage and for our relationship.

Here is the great blessing: Ron now preaches all over the country and *I have total veto power* over his travel plans for Acquire the Fire events. That means I can say, "Honey, I don't want you to go that many times this year," or "I don't want you to go this weekend, because important things will be happening here at home." Ron has given me the authority to do that, and I am blown away by God's graciousness and His favor on my life because of this. My husband has given me the respect to trust me with that power. But it is only because I let him go, only because I laid it down before the Lord and adopted the vision God gave him.

"If you're his Number One Critic, it won't help you at all." Really, can we make things better by complaining? Have you ever known it to work?

Let's suppose he's got the vision, and he calls home to report on all the marvelous things God is doing in the ministry. You're angry, though, because he's not home. You're angry because he didn't call earlier, or didn't call more, or didn't . . . whatever. Will it help you to complain and criticize? If God is building him up, and teenagers are thanking him for his ministry to them, and you pull him down over the phone, will he want to call again just as soon as he can? Will he be itching to report to you as soon as possible, to share and relate and be mutually encouraged?

Or will he avoid his Number One Critic?

We have to bite our tongues during those challenging times when he is more involved in the ministry than we are. We need to give him more encouragement than anyone else, be his Number One Fan. That way, our presence becomes a haven for him, our voice becomes the music of encouragement in his ears, the foretaste of loving arms that he looks forward to feeling ASAP!

I can hear you say, "Well, Katie, what if he is indeed neglecting me and my feelings? What do I do then?" The answer is, pray. And when he is home, you lighten up and adore him. It's not easy, but if you go to God with your

We need to give him more encouragement than anyone else, be his Number One Fan.

needs, He will give you the unconditional love that no person on earth could ever provide. Yes, God will answer your prayer because He wants you both to work as a team.

I have prayed that our home would be full of peace, a haven for my husband. I make it clean and orderly and beautiful and . . . fun. I push back the all-too-natural chaos with pretty music and candles and cleanliness. I am the manager of my home, as a sacrifice of praise and thanksgiving to the Lord. Amazingly, all of this melts Ron's heart in his love for me.

I want Ron out there and going, because God has called him to do it. (I even told him, "I can't imagine you being gone *less* than you are now. How could the work get done?") Yes, I want him out there, but I want him home with me, too. This is the key: when he's home, *I want him home with me in his heart.*

"You might have to hem and haw for a while." Many of us with ministry husbands will need to learn how to speak and teach too. For example, I speak to our intern girls and sometimes speak at Acquire the Fire conferences. I love it because it's a time when I can pour into other people what God has been pouring into me.

Speaking is so vital because through your words you establish God's kingdom in people's hearts. When God gave your husband the vision, He gave it to you as well, because you are one. It is likely that you will be expected to teach. Now that puts fear and trembling in some of us. But if you will take hold of Scripture and speak it over yourself, God can change your heart about that fear. You can speak with confidence and authority.

If you aren't used to it, you'll shake a little bit, your mouth will go dry, and your palms will get wet. You'll hem and haw. But your heart will shine through. Your love for God will be evident, and that is what will be conveyed. So just keep doing it and know by faith that you are really establishing the kingdom of God in hungry hearts. Here are some Scriptures to help you:

> *God did not give us a spirit of timidity, but a spirit of power, of love and of self-discipline.*
>
> —2 Timothy 1:7

> *The LORD said to me, "Do not say, 'I am only a child.' You must go to everyone I send you to and say whatever I command you. Do not be afraid of them, for I am with you and will rescue you," declares the LORD.*
>
> *Then the LORD reached out his hand and touched my mouth and said to me, "Now, I have put my words in your mouth."*
>
> —Jeremiah 1:7–9

> *The Sovereign LORD has given me an instructed tongue, to know the word that sustains the weary. He wakens me morning by morning, wakens my ear to listen like one being taught. The Sovereign LORD has opened my ears, and I have not been rebellious; I have not drawn back.*
>
> —Isaiah 50:4–5

I am the manager of my home, as a sacrifice of praise and thanksgiving to the Lord.

"I have put my words in your mouth and covered you with the shadow of my hand—I who set the heavens in place, who laid the foundations of the earth, and who say to Zion, 'You are my people.'"

—Isaiah 51:16

Feel better? I'm sure you can find many more encouraging Scriptures as you edge toward those fearful waters of speaking and teaching in public. And I know you will be amazed at how God uses you. You will be amazed because, with your humble heart, God will show Himself strong on your behalf. (And if you think you're hot and have it all together, the Lord will help with that, too.) Just humble yourself before Him; He'll lift you up and use you in love and service. Thanks be to God!

I know you will be amazed at how God uses you. You will be amazed because, with your humble heart, God will show Himself strong on your behalf.

CHAPTER SEVEN

Avoiding the Ragged Edge

I came across a startling quotation the other day: "The world is run by tired people." Is that true, I wondered? Then I realized how I could definitely make it into a true statement: "The *church* is run by tired *ministers.*"

Sad, but true. People who want to change the world don't get very much sleep. Yet the Scriptures paint a different vision.

> *God is not a God of disorder but of peace. As in all the congregations of the saints . . . everything should be done in a fitting and orderly way.*
>
> —1 Corinthians 14:33, 40

If we're walking around fried, frazzled, and fatigued, is God pleased?

Paul is speaking of worship practices in this passage, but the principle holds true in general: God does things in peaceful, orderly ways. We can look at the stars and the planets, how things perfectly circle and rotate, and we see an orderly Creator. In fact, in any area of creation we see the orderly hand of our God at work. In His commands to the church, too, God calls us to be people of peace and order.

If we're walking around fried, frazzled, and fatigued, is God pleased? If we're constantly ragged and barely limping along, will we be an encouraging presence in the ministry? And if we constantly stretch ourselves too thin, how can we claim to offer people "life, and life more abundantly"? The dark circles under our eyes belie our message every time.

I can't tell you how many times I've had youth pastors come to me after an event and ask, "Ron, how do I keep from running myself into the ground? How do I organize my personal life so I'm not so ragged in the ministry?"

The initial response is to think. Think carefully. Why is it that we live such frazzled lives?

TIME WASTERS ARE WASTING US!

For one thing, we fill our lives with time wasters. But we don't call them time wasters; we call them "letting down"—indulging in things like television, movies, and ball games. These are things that are making noise in our lives, and they suck our lives away. Yes, I feel as if, when I sit in front of the tube, there's a giant vacuum cleaner sucking the life out of me. It's sucking my brains, my time, my potential, all the things I could be dreaming of and praying for.

These are indeed time wasters, because I'm letting somebody else have an adventure for me, letting them enjoy the adventure that I never get around to experiencing for myself.

"Come on, Ron!" you say. "We need to chill sometimes."

I know that. But wouldn't it be much better to have some fun with your kids, for instance? One of the things I love to do is wrestle with my kids. Sometimes I just tickle them, close my eyes, and listen to them laugh. Have you listened to the innocence of a child laughing his heart out lately? That's not a waste of time; it's standing under a waterfall of peace.

But we say, "After this movie then I'll work," or "After this next thing," or "After this ball game and then . . ." I'm all for watching a good game now and then. But could we be a little more alert to that sucking sound?

WE JUST CAN'T SAY "NO!"

You hear, "Oh, can you help with this?" Then what do you answer? Have you learned yet that somebody else's sudden little crisis is not necessarily your immediate emergency? We need to learn to say "no" to off-the-cuff requests. We need to learn the difference between the important and the merely urgent.

Of course, we don't want to hurt anyone's feelings. But assertiveness can be carried out with all due respect and appropriate tact. It just takes some practice. Try standing in front of the mirror for a few minutes each day and practice saying:

Hmm, sorry, but I'm already booked for that time slot.
No, I've already blocked out that time for family.

Saying "no" means not letting others control your time.

I'm afraid I can't; I've scheduled that time for
another matter.
No, my policy is never to . . .
No, that wouldn't be the best use of my time right now.
No.

You get the idea. The more you practice, the less fearful these kinds of phrases will become. You need to learn them well to stay sharp in ministry.

Just the other day one of our interns e-mailed me, "This lady called and is thinking about coming to Acquire the Fire. She wants to talk to you about it." I e-mailed him back and told him to have her talk to his supervisor. Why? As much as I'd like to, I can't talk to every person who wants to talk to me. I'm guessing that you're in a similar situation. So set those boundaries. It's an essential form of "no" for all of us. It requires having competent people around you, of course, who can screen your calls and stand in for you when needed. Then say "no" and delegate. Otherwise, instead of effectiveness we end up with busyness.

The problem is, we think we have a full life because we're doing this and we're doing that. But being busy is not a sign of being effective. Engaging in more and more activities usually means we know less and less of our families, of ourselves, of our God. This isn't good.

Saying no means not letting others control your time. You set your time and your agenda based on what you know is your vision for your family, vision for your ministry, and vision for your own spiritual growth. This doesn't mean you don't allow for diversions from time to time. But that's why you raise up other people around you to be able to handle things. Then you can say, as the leader, "No, if there are other people who can do that, let them do it."

VISIONLESS, WE'RE FRAZZLED

If you have no vision for your own personal development, that's a prime ragged-edge producer!

"I want to grow in the Lord and be a better leader," you say. "And I want to change the world." Good. But here's the point: only if you're driven by a vision will you be able to prioritize the steps and stick to the things you need to accomplish for overall effectiveness. *I need to read this much Bible; I need to spend this much time reading other relevant material; I need to spend this time going to these seminars, seeing these people, doing these things.* When you don't have a vision driving you, you tend to do things—perhaps many things—without purpose. You get involved in activity for activity's sake. And so you get totally frazzled.

You also need a real vision for your family and for your marriage. We've explored this in the previous two chapters, but I'd like to add an important point here: agree with your spouse about the amount of time you will spend at work versus the time you spend with your family. You can't say, "Honey, I've got a job, and I'm a volunteer youth pastor, and I have to do both those things. So I'll come home and eat and stuff, from time to time . . ."

No, family comes first. When we first started the Teen Mania ministry, I said, "Katie, I want you to know that I don't really believe in a 40-hour work week, but according to this Western mind-set, 40 hours is what people are supposed

If you have no vision for your own personal development, that's a prime ragged-edge producer!

to work. So the only time that I feel belongs to me, that I feel I could fully give to the ministry, is 40 hours a week. Anything outside of 40, I am going to ask you for permission to work." We have agreement about this,because I'm not going to do whatever I want to do and drag her through life with the occasional guilt-inducing, "But God cares about all those people, don't *you*?"

Don't get me wrong, I definitely work more than 40 hours per week, but Katie and I agree on it in advance. We plan out our family times. Any time outside the 40 hours does not come out of our family times, but out of my discretionary time. What do I mean by that? Well, the time hanging out with other guys, TV, movies, sleep . . . all that is discretionary. I can cut into that all I want to work for the ministry. I will not cut into the family time.

It's not our right to drag our spouses through life saying, "But God told me." We are a team in this thing. We are one unit, one family, and if God told you, He can tell your spouse, too. It's more important to have unity than to have your own way when it comes to time.

I also refuse to do things that infringe on our trust. For example, sometimes opportunities come our way that are outside the bounds of our time agreement. Usually, I don't even tell Katie about those; I just pass them up. However, occasionally I might say, "Honey, do you think we could do this? Do you think I could travel here? I'm only going to do this if you agree." Since I don't ask this very often, she knows that if I do it must be something we should really pray about and consider.

NOT HEARING FROM GOD, WE GET CONFUSED

Once you have an agreement with your spouse about time demands of ministry and home, then you need to think about your time with God. Organizing your personal life has to start with that. Are you really connected with God as you carry out your ministry? Are you hearing from Him every day? If not, what's the point?

Your relationship with God is what fuels your ministry, so time with Him has to be the highlight of your day. "Man, I can't wait until tomorrow morning and my quiet time with God!" It's the thing that keeps you kicking, keeps you excited for life itself.

Make it a profitable time. Include some diligent study, and always be learning. A story is told about John Wesley, the great 17th-century revivalist, field preacher, and scholar. He once received a note that said: "The Lord told me to tell you that He doesn't need your book-learning, your Greek and your Hebrew."

Wesley answered, "Thank you, sir. Your letter was superfluous, however, as I already knew the Lord has no need for my 'book-learning,' as you put it. However, although the Lord has not directed me to say so, on my own responsibility I would like to say to you that the Lord does not need your ignorance, either."

We need not be frazzled in ministry. But to avoid becoming one of those "tired ministers" who run the church, we've got to slow down, learn to draw our energy from the rest that God gives us. I leave you with how Pastor Mike Breen puts it in his LifeShapes seminars:

If we're to understand how we're to continue, we need to know how we are started. How did we get this thing

Your relationship with God is what fuels your ministry, so time with Him has to be the highlight of your day.

going? Or, more to the point, how did God get this thing going?

Well, He made us on the sixth day, and after a busy day being created, we spend the next day resting. We're made for work. We're made for fruitfulness. We're made for productive activity. But our very first whole day experience is what? Rest. So, here's the first little piece of revelation about the rhythm of life that God wants us to invest in.

We work from rest, not rest from work. Human beings are designed to work. But they're designed to work from a place of rest. Not to crash into rest from too much work.[1]

---

1. Mike Breen, *Living in Rhythm with Life Teaching DVD* (Colorado Springs, CO: Cook Communications Ministries, 2006).

CHAPTER EIGHT

Stay Saturated!

After a pouring rain, I noticed a water leak in my office, a little one, just over the windowsill. I couldn't tell where it originated, because of the ceiling tiles, so I set a garbage can on the sill to catch the tiny drops. It was an annoyance, but it wasn't enough to flood me or wreck the furniture. It was a drip; but I certainly wasn't saturated.

However, during the Christmas break recently we experienced a different kind of leak in one of our dormitories. I think it occurred right on Christmas Day over that weekend. A two-inch pipe froze and broke, and no one was there to notice it for two days.

The leak sprung on the second floor, and it flooded the

**Think about "the greatest possible
amount"—so full that there is
no way to hold any more.
What would it be like to
know God that way?**

floor below—all the walls, all the desks and beds, all the
carpets. It dripped down everywhere. What a mess!

We hired professionals to dry everything out, and it
was an amazing thing to observe. They drilled holes at the
bottom of all the walls, inserted hoses attached to big air
blowers, and blew air into the walls for many days. They
also set up a huge dehumidifier to pull out 25 gallons of
moisture a day!

That's more than a drip. The place was saturated. But
what does *saturation* really mean?

> *to soak;*
> *to fill;*
> *to load to capacity;*
> *to cause a substance to unite with the greatest possible*
>   *amount of another substance;*
> *to cause to combine until there is no further tendency to*
>   *combine.*

Think about "the greatest possible amount"—so full
that there is no way to hold any more. What would it be like
to know God that way? To be saturated with Him?

Actually, we're saturated with lots of things these
days, aren't we? Some of us are saturated with sports; we
know all the teams and statistics, and we can't wait for the
next game to begin. Others are saturated with movies, or

music, the Internet, or television sitcoms. Some are saturated with news, so they're glued to CNN or Fox every minute of the day. "Suppose I missed the latest headline!" they think. It sends chills up their spines. (I have to be careful here; I, too, love to know what's going on in the world.)

There's nothing inherently wrong with most of the things that grab our interest. Many of them can be enjoyed as gifts from God. But saturation? It's too easy to be a servant of God and still saturate ourselves with things other *than* God. In fact, whatever completely permeates our lives—isn't that really our God?

How then, with such busy lives, can we be saturated with God? Let me suggest this: *We could start by making our personal space a God-friendly environment.*

CREATE A GOD-FRIENDLY LIFE

We talk a lot about user-friendliness. What about a God-friendly environment in our own personal lives? It would be an environment where God finds it easy to hang out, where He would smile and say, "I like that. I'm going to show up here some more." Imagine! The kind of life space where God says, "That's where I want to be."

We have seeker-sensitive services, but what about God-friendly services? And how about a God-friendly life?

In the same way that we can choose the nature of our "personal space" whether we're driving in a car or sitting in a restaurant, we can create a space in our lives that will delight God's heart and invite His presence. How can we do that?

Start by making our personal space a God-friendly environment.

Jump in the tub. Don't stand under a thin trickle where you have to bounce around to get wet.

Start your saturation first thing in the morning. Jump in the tub. Don't stand under a thin trickle where you have to bounce around to get wet. Isn't that what some of our quiet times are like? Here's a little Scripture, a little prayer. *Whoa, I got a drop, so I'm good to go.* No; dive in!

Psalm 63 speaks of "following hard after" God, seeking Him with all our heart. Psalm 5 tells us to come early in the morning and seek Him. Even Jesus, the Son of God, rose very early in the morning, while it was still dark, to go and hang out with His Father. If Jesus felt it necessary to "dive in" like that, how much more should we feel the need?

Some people say, "But I'm not a morning person!" No problem. You can saturate in the evening. Jesus worked ministry late into the night, too, then He got up early and had time with His father. Why? Because He wanted to be saturated.

This is a life pattern that says, "God, I really want to connect with You! Feed me, feed me! I don't want to just read a little verse and a poem; I have to get some food." We must get on our faces and say, "I love You, Lord. You are God." We have to really submerge ourselves in worship.

Invite the tsunami of God's presence to hit you. The great tsunami of December 2004 was 60 feet high when it hit Sri Lanka, Sumatra, and so many other nations. Entire villages were washed away. Some people who lived in concrete houses survived, while their neighbors, living in huts, perished. Things that were stable and built solidly gave refuge.

When you invite the God-tsunami to hit, realize that all of the things not built on a firm foundation are going to be washed away. Sometimes we become very comfortable with our huts and habits, the ways of our comfortable lifestyle. There are things we like to do and things we like to see. When God "hits," it's as if He says, "If you really want my presence, then all of the things built with straw and stubble will need to be washed away."

Invite the tsunami to hit, but realize that God is constantly inviting us to come up to the mountain with Him. We will definitely need to leave some things behind for our own good. *Drop the weight and baggage to get where I am.*

Without a doubt, if we choose to walk with the Lord, there will be a demand on our lives. We will have less of the world, less of our own ego. If we want more of His presence, His tangible saturation, then more of the flesh must go.

It is so easy, after you have been with God a while, to think, "I am a pretty decent person, and God must be pleased with me compared to my neighbor over there." But this isn't a competition. God works with each of us wherever we are. He starts there and grows us as we open ourselves to His sanctifying Spirit. Are we closer to Him than the next guy? That's not the question; the real question is: am I closer to God at the moment than I was a moment ago? It's a matter of keeping an open heart.

Are we satisfied with being just a little damp? Or shall we get drenched? God sets higher standards for us the longer we are Christians. We are supposed to go from glory to glory.

I want to know Christ and the power of his resurrection and the fellowship of sharing in his sufferings, becoming like him in his death, and so, somehow, to attain to the

God sets higher standards for us the longer we are Christians. We are supposed to go from glory to glory.

> *resurrection from the dead.*
>
> *Not that I have already obtained all this, or have already been made perfect, but I press on to take hold of that for which Christ Jesus took hold of me. Brothers, I do not consider myself yet to have taken hold of it. But one thing I do: Forgetting what is behind and straining toward what is ahead, I press on toward the goal to win the prize for which God has called me heavenward in Christ Jesus.*
>
> *All of us who are mature should take such a view of things. And if on some point you think differently, that too God will make clear to you. Only let us live up to what we have already attained.*
>
> —Philippians 3:10–16

Press on! Invite the tsunami to hit, but realize some of the cherished huts will be washed away.

Realize it's bigger than you. That is, realize this thing called the presence of God is an amazing experience worthy of all reverence and awe. The psalmist says, "The LORD confides in those who fear him; he makes his covenant known to them" (Ps. 25:14). God will show us secrets; He'll show us what He's really like. He will whisper and give us insight into the deep things of His nature—if we respect Him enough to listen.

If there is any focus that the Christian leader of the

future will need, it is the discipline of dwelling in the presence of the One who keeps asking us, "Do you love me? Do you love me? Do you love me?" It is the discipline of contemplative prayer. Through contemplative prayer we can keep ourselves from being pulled from one urgent issue to another and from becoming stranger to our own and God's heart. Contemplative prayer keeps us home, rooted and safe, even when we are on the road, moving from place to place, and often surrounded by sounds of violence and war. Contemplative prayer deepens in us the knowledge that we . . . already belong to God, even though everything and everyone around us keeps suggesting the opposite.

From Henri J. M. Nouwen, *In the Name of Jesus* (New York: Crossroad, 1989)

This kind of prayer is a listening attitude that waits in the presence of the awesomeness of the sovereign Lord. Some haven't heard from this Lord in so long, yet if we aren't sensing His presence, then we might ask whether we truly honor and fear Him as we ought.

My son Cameron was reading through the Bible, and he came to me about one particular story. In that passage, the fire of the Lord came and filled the temple after Solomon prayed and dedicated it to God. Cameron said, "Think about how much they must have honored the Lord for Him to show up like that!" I thought, *Lord, I want to honor You like that.*

He will whisper and give us insight into the deep things of His nature—if we respect Him enough to listen.

We marinate in God until we taste like Him. Meditate upon God's Word until all the flavor sinks in.

Marinate until you're flavored. I could speak of "meditating," but I would rather call it marinating. That is, we marinate in God until we taste like Him. It's a marvelous analogy, isn't it? Meditate upon God's Word until all the flavor sinks in.

What a contrast to checking off the Scriptures we're memorizing! Could we marinate in those words, too, until we begin to take on their godly characteristics? I have enjoyed a whole new season of meditating on Scripture over the last several months, and I'm amazed at what's happening to my mind. The thoughts of God are becoming my thoughts . . . naturally, like second nature. Is there a greater blessing in life?

Scripture abounds with invitations to marinate . . .

This book of the law shall not depart out of thy mouth;
but thou shalt meditate therein day and night, that thou
mayest observe to do according to all that is written
therein: for then thou shalt make thy way prosperous,
and then thou shalt have good success.
—Joshua 1:8 (KJV)

Blessed is the man that walketh not in the counsel of the
ungodly, nor standeth in the way of sinners, nor sitteth
in the seat of the scornful. But his delight is in the law of
the LORD; and in his law doth he meditate day and night.
—Psalm 1:1–2 (KJV)

I will meditate in thy precepts, and have respect unto thy ways.
> —Psalm 119:15 (KJV)

My hands also will I lift up unto thy commandments, which I have loved; and I will meditate in thy statutes.
> —Psalm 119:48 (KJV)

I remember the days of old; I meditate on all thy works; I muse on the work of thy hands.
> —Psalm 143:5 (KJV)

Meditate upon these things; give thyself wholly to them; that thy profiting may appear to all.
> —1 Timothy 4:15 (KJV)

What would a little marinating do for the rest of your day? How would it change what happens between your praise sessions? Ephesians 6 talks about prayer without ceasing. It really is walking in communion with a very personal God.

CONSIDER YOUR MOTIVE

But why? Why should we do all of this? It would be easy just to say, "Do this, and you will have more peace, more joy, a much better life." That would be true, but the fact is that most things we hear preached today are self-centered. It's about us, what we want and what we'll get.

No! It's all about God. What He wants and what He gets. Otherwise, we are no different from the local humanists. Humanism says the goal of life is for humans to be happy. When that penetrates our Gospel, when we are following the rules just to keep from going to hell, then we have actually moved far away from the Gospel.

Why should we saturate ourselves in God's presence

He is worthy of every morsel of my mind, my being, and my lifestyle.

or live a lifestyle that will invite His friendship? Because *He is worthy of every morsel of my mind, my being, and my lifestyle.* He is worth the price that Jesus paid on the cross for me. And He deserves all that was bought there. He is worth all that I am, 24/7, until the day I die.

I could never repay Him, of course, but He is worth it all. If I never received one blessing, if I had no more joy and no more peace than anyone else, God would still be worth every amount of mental, spiritual, and physical energy that I have. He deserves nothing less. Clearly, then, the reason for staying saturated in Him is that it's an act of worship that He deserves in every way.

It is also the reason for all our outreach, at home and abroad. Jesus paid on the cross for the sins of the world— even if we preach, and no one ever says yes. All people we try to reach are sinners just like us, and, like us, they don't deserve salvation. But when Jesus gave His life, He offered Himself, the perfect sacrifice, for all mankind. A God-centered life and motive says, "You paid for them all; You deserve them all." Doesn't He deserve everything that He paid for? Therefore, our motive for outreach is: Christ deserves the reward of His sacrifice.

Let our motives be pure, in saturating ourselves and in reaching out to others. As a Youth Specialist, you will often face people you don't have a heart for. But do you have a heart for God? Whether or not you have a heart for those particular people or not, He paid the price for them. It is about pleasing Him and proclaiming His message. He is worth our all.

Our job is to go and tell a world of people about Who really owns them. So many teens you'll invite to your youth group will have rough edges and tons of character flaws. You might not like them very much. No matter. God sent His Son to die for them; He is worthy of all their hearts, all their souls for the rest of their lives. Our job is to help them see that. And really, is there a better job in the whole world?

A God-centered life and motive says, "You paid for them all; You deserve them all."

CHAPTER NINE

The Message of the Youth Specialist

This may be the most important chapter of the book series. Thus far, we've discussed how to build a thriving youth ministry from the ground up with tried-and-true principles using lots of stories to illustrate the effectiveness of this paradigm. We've talked about the personal life of the Youth Specialist and the demands God puts on us.

But once we've built the ministry, and we've got our lifestyle in order, what is it that we are actually here to preach? The core of our message is critically important for a number of reasons. Despite all that has been done in the name of Christ for youth ministry, and all that's been done for the sake of ministry in general in America, we still have a morally bankrupt society.

Despite all that has been done in the name of Christ for youth ministry, and all that's been done for the sake of ministry in general in America, we still have a morally bankrupt society.

Considering the number of megachurches, TV ministries, radio ministries, printed matter, different translations of the Bible (to say nothing of the multiple Bibles most Christians have stored in their closets), as well as some 5,600 new Christian books published each year, why is it that we live in a culture where there is more divorce; more pornography; more demonstrative, arrogant, bold sinning than ever before? How could those two trends co-exist *unless the message proclaimed is either the wrong message or it is not penetrating deeply enough to change convictions in the heart of the hearer?*

If we work to rescue a generation, we'd better make sure the message we are proclaiming is the message that produces radical life-change in the hearts of every person that hears it.

What follows is a summary of what I believe are the absolutely non-negotiable imperatives (no matter which branch of Christianity you might come from) for producing the change the Bible refers to. To see a generation won to Christ and be swept off its feet, and to see our teens become a real, vibrant witness to this world, we'd better make sure we include the following:

TOTAL AND COMPLETE COMMITMENT

Do not soft-sell what the Gospel asks of us. Phrases like, "All you have to do is pray this little prayer," mislead people and misrepresent Christ. We use so many words, phrases, and concepts that are actually unbiblical in our asking people to come to Christ. We say, "Do you want to accept Christ?" Someone please show me where that is said in the Bible. There is only one place in one translation that I have ever found that even alluded to "accepting Christ."

In normal English vernacular, we don't even use the word "accept" that way, yet in ministry we use it to say, "Do you want to somehow get connected to God?" in the same way we'd say, "Do you *accept* Visa?" or, "Do you *accept* MasterCard?" Is this what we're talking about?

The word "accept" also has weak overtones. We'll ask, "Will someone accept John, because we all know no one really loves him?" Is that what Jesus is? Someone with no self-esteem who needs our acceptance? *Please accept Him into your heart.* When we ask people to come to Jesus in this way we end up with a mentality that produces *passive Christians at best.*

People in church also say, "Have you received the Lord?" It's true that in John 1 you'll find the word "receive": "To those who receive Him, He gave power to become the sons of God." But the word "receive" in the Greek means, "to embrace or hold on to." The way we communicate it, it sounds more like a passive word. *If you bring people to Christ in a passive way, they will remain passive Christians their whole lives.*

Have you heard someone say, "Do you want to have a personal relationship with Jesus Christ?" Nowhere in the Bible do I see Jesus asking us to enter a personal relationship with Him. Obviously when we make Jesus the center of our lives, we embrace Him as our Master and our King. We get

Do not soft-sell what the Gospel asks of us.

If you bring people to Christ in a passive way, they will remain passive Christians their whole lives.

a very personal, very close relationship because He lives inside us. You can't get any closer than that.

All of these phrases substitute watered-down rhetoric for the reality of what being a Christian really is: total and complete surrender to Jesus Christ. Here in America, we embrace a kind of "cultural Christianity" that looks at total surrender as "radical" or "untamed." People think, "Well, I'm not a Muslim; I'm not a Jew; I guess I'm a Christian." Those raised in church end up inoculated against a totally-sold-out message of the Gospel.

I've stopped asking people if they want to become a Christian. Jesus never asked anybody if they wanted to be a Christian. People were called Christians because they followed Christ and imitated Him. It was actually the secular world that first came up with the idea, "Hey, let's call them Christians." Now I ask people if they would like to become a "follower of Christ." Thirty-two different times, Jesus mentioned the phrase, "Follow me." We are not called to be Christians but to follow Him in our hearts, with our lifestyles, with our actions, and with our motives. One day we'll follow Him to heaven as devoted followers.

In Matthew 16, Jesus said, "If anyone would come after me, he must deny himself and take up his cross and follow me." Denying ourselves means to give up our selfish ambitions, our selfish drives, our selfish desires, and our selfish lifestyles.

Compare this to *enlisting* in the army. Enlisting is a lot

different than joining. Following Jesus is a lot different from "just pray this simple prayer with me." When you enlist, you sign on the dotted line. You sign over the ownership of your life and you are no longer in charge. This is the kind of challenge that Jesus laid out in the Gospel. This is the kind of challenge we must lay out if we are to become real followers of Him.

In addition to totally enlisting, we need to make sure that we are not simply providing "fire insurance"—offering people an escape from hell. We can scare them out of hell. But they end up making a foxhole decision just to avoid pain or punishment, rather than to run to Christ with their whole hearts. There is a big difference between running from hell and running to Christ.

We don't want bare-minimum Christians, yet our altar call says, "If you want to come to Christ, *all you have to do . . .*" How dare we cheapen grace that way? All you have to do is turn your back on the world, take up your cross, and follow Him. All you have to do is change your lifestyle, change your heart, and change the direction of everything you are.

The Bible says He rewards those who diligently seek Him. As we call people to Christ, we need to make sure they become God-seekers, God-lovers, and God-followers. The psalmist says, "As the deer pants for streams of water, so my soul pants for you, O God" (Ps. 42:1). We want to produce a world of young people who turn to Christ, follow Him, and yearn for the deep things of God all the days of their lives.

As Youth Specialists, I would recommend we NEVER, EVER, EVER use these overused, inaccurate, unbiblical, and

I ask people if they would like to become a "follower of Christ."

As we call people to Christ, we need to make sure they become God-seekers, God-lovers, and God-followers.

misunderstood phrases when asking people to come to Christ:

- Do you want to accept Christ?
- Do you want to receive Him as your Lord and Savior?
- Do you want a personal relationship with Christ?
- Do you want Him to save you?
- All you have to do is pray this simple prayer with me . . .

Instead, once you have painted a picture that Jesus is really worth giving your all to, invite young people to become followers of Christ with phrases like:

- Are you ready to turn away from the world and its lies and come running to Jesus?
- Will you enlist in His army today, signing away your life to do whatever He wants?
- Would you like to have the miracle of a new heart? Jesus called it being born again, and only He can give it. But to get it you must turn away from the world.

With this kind of appeal, there may be fewer people coming to the front to pray, but at least they will become real followers of Christ. Who cares how many are crying their eyes out at every altar call we give if it is only emotion and not true conversion?

WHAT KIND OF CHRISTIAN ARE WE PRODUCING?

Once we have asked young people to enlist, asked them to give their all, now we need to think deeply about who they are to become. I'll use the metaphor of the military once again. When people enlist in the military, the boot camp process is a total stripping down of their civilian identity. The military changes their hair, clothes, and puts them through pain to strip away their old habits. They receive a whole new set of clothes, habits, and a new lifestyle. So it must be with us, as we begin to help young people form their new identity as followers of Christ.

Just like in the military, Christ-followers, too, have a code of conduct: the Bible. It doesn't guarantee that we'll be perfect, but it does tell us what things a Christian *should* be marked by.

Devotion. God is looking for people who are marked by devotion. They don't just shout that they love Jesus; they are so devoted to Him they'll follow Him to the death. It doesn't matter if the circumstances are hard or easy. They will follow Him until the end. Even if He doesn't answer another prayer, they will stay devoted because they love Him so much, and He has already done so much for them.

Defiance. We need to produce young people that live in defiance of the enemy's tactics. That love what is true and hate what is sinful. Too many people that call themselves Christians still love the world. The Bible clearly tells us that

Who cares how many are crying their eyes out at every altar call we give if it is only emotion, and not true conversion?

God is looking for people who are marked by devotion.

"friendship with the world is hatred toward God" (Jas. 4:4). The mere fact that we have to beg them not to listen to secular music or watch these programs shows that in their heart of hearts they still love the world and are attracted to it. They are letting the world entertain and coddle them. We need to teach teens to see through the lies no matter how cool the music or movies might be. We must teach them that they are being brainwashed with lies and must turn away from anything that contradicts the truth of the Bible.

Courage. Most people who call themselves Christians look more like cowards than courageous followers of Christ. They give in whenever they are confronted about their faith. They give in whenever temptations are presented to them. They are not like the men and women of old who stood for their faith even though it could cost them their lives or limbs. Martyrs like Polycarp were burned at the stake and yet kept praising God despite their persecution. We need to produce young people with backbone. We must show them that because of what Jesus did for us, and the courage He demonstrated on the cross, we can do the same. Jesus showed us how to be courageous.

Endurance. This is one of the lost evidences of our faith. People don't endure a workout program, a diet, or even marriages. The most supposedly sacred commitment in our society is not endured very long. In fact, today many couples have changed their wedding vows from "till death do us part" to "for as long as our love shall last." (At least they're being honest.)

People say, "Lord, I will die for You. I will do anything

for You." But when it rains on Sunday, they don't go to church because they might get their hair messed up. We need to produce young people who are fit to endure. Who are battle-tested and have put on the armor of God, and are ready to fight the good fight of faith.

Jesus taught us how to endure as He went to His death with silent dignity. In six hours of hanging on the cross (after being whipped and tortured and spit on and beat up, with a crown of thorns shoved into His head), Jesus was utterly silent with the exception of about one minute's worth of speech. In the silence, He screams a message to us, *"This is what it looks like to endure."* He saw the joy set before Him. This is the kind of Christ-follower we as Youth Specialists are called to produce.

CHRIST-FOLLOWERS ARE GROWTH-ORIENTED

When someone joins the army or the navy, it's natural to anticipate progressing up through the ranks. What soldier would want to enlist as a private, and 20 years later still be a private? Yet we have churches full of privates who haven't progressed a step in 20 or 30 years. Perhaps they think they have made a decision and since they're going to heaven they have no obligation to do anything else. Let's be sure we give our young people the paradigm that *once enlisted, there are a lot of ranks to grow into:* There's basic training. There's advanced training. There are special ops. There are covert ops. There are all kinds of places you can advance in

We must teach them that they are being brainwashed with lies and must turn away from anything that contradicts the truth of the Bible.

We need to produce young people with backbone. We must show them that because of what Jesus did for us, and the courage He demonstrated on the cross, we can do the same.

the Kingdom and grow in your faith.

I recently talked to a young man in the army. He said that when you enlist as an E-1, after two or three years you can get promoted to E-4 without doing much of anything. All you have to do is be there, do your time, and you automatically advance. After E-4, if you want to move on to sergeant level, you have to study. You have to go through special training and prove yourself.

We often see people slip into church as an E-1 and then slide into E-4 without any effort, but there they remain. They never do more than just show up on Sunday and then wonder *why* they are going nowhere in their faith. We need to help young people see that growth and training is a natural part of being a follower of Christ. To have an "illustrious" career in the things of God, you must increase in rank and continue to grow.

WE ARE DISCIPLES SO THAT THEY CAN DISCIPLE OTHERS

In Western Christianity, we have built the kingdom of God one person at a time rather than multiplying the growth *exponentially*. Jesus taught exponential growth: all the disciples made other disciples who made other disciples and so on.

There is an example of this level of discipleship in Bogotá, Colombia, where a church of 120,000 people and a youth group of 40,000 trains their members to make disciples. This is a natural part of Christianity.

We need to think in terms of multiplying, not just adding, and so do our teens. So often, we treat discipleship as if it were optional. Instead, we should train our young people to think that they too need to win people and disciple them. They need to pass on what they have learned.

If everyone in your youth group reached four or ten people this year, how big would that be? Think exponentially. Train your kids to multiply themselves. When you do, you will give them a priceless jewel that they will treasure the rest of their lives. Your teens will continue to perpetuate the kingdom of God long after they have grown up and moved away and gotten married.

WORLD CONQUEST IS IN OUR DNA

People join an army because they know that there is a war to win. Part of our drawing people to Christ is helping them understand they have left the army of darkness and have joined the army of Light. Jesus said in Matthew 11:12: "From the days of John the Baptist until now, the kingdom of heaven has been forcefully advancing, and forceful men lay hold of it." Part of the natural course as a soldier in the army of Light is to help forcefully advance the Kingdom. This message that has changed us so deeply and so profoundly cannot be kept to ourselves. The One who died on the cross is worthy of proclaiming to the ends of the earth.

Understand it's not an extracurricular activity to share your faith with your friends; it's a fundamental part of the job description, part of your life. It's not an extracurricular

Jesus taught us how to endure as He went to his death with silent dignity.

Jesus taught exponential growth: all the disciples made other disciples who made other disciples and so on.

activity to go on a mission trip in the summertime. It's part of your DNA, what you're made of. It's what you're going to do for the rest of your life.

Why? Because *that is what a soldier does.* A soldier goes to win the war, to win the battle at hand. Right now in North America we are entrenched in the battle for this generation. We have to train our young people that they are marching into battle. They are marching into war. What is the strategy they need to use each day, each week? We've got to train our teens that there is a war for souls all around the world with the Hindu, Muslims, tribal people, atheists, and Buddhists. People are lost, and it's our job as soldiers of the King to get this message to the ends of the earth.

Jesus said, "This gospel of the kingdom will be preached in the whole world as a testimony to all nations, and then the end will come" (Matt. 24:14). It's our job to make soldiers who will fulfill this commission. Jesus fully intends and expects for us as His representatives to accomplish this goal. It is not optional. It's not just for the radicals. It's for the normal follower of Christ.

After all the work is said and done, let's make sure our message is potent and produces a life change. We are helping our teens go somewhere in their faith so they can share it with others. We can get the job done—reach this generation, reach the world, and bring a smile to our Father's face. That is the job of every Youth Specialist.

Great Commission Competition

By Jeanne Mayo

I. THE PURPOSE

Every youth ministry needs seasons of strong, fresh growth. A format like the "Great Commission Competition" can do incredible things to jump-start growth and fresh energy in your youth ministry.

II. THE OVERALL PLAN

Competition is a part of every teenager's life. Thus, the Great Commission Competition takes the motivation of competition and places it within a positive and Christ-honoring framework. Teams are formulated among the youth group, and they compete against each other for three months (12 youth services). Points are given for three things only: (1) bringing guests, (2) getting guests to return for four weeks, and (3) keeping the "regulars" attending.

The first prize needs to be a trip of some sort that will excite the members of the group. We have done everything from taking trips to Disney World to winter ski trips. Trips are not nearly as expensive as you might think; you can cut down on costs by driving wherever you go. I get adults from the church to underwrite the cost of the trip before the competition even launches. (Approximate the cost of the trip and divide it into 5–10 parts. Then approach 5–10 individuals in the church and present your vision for reaching more youth in your community. Explain The Great Commission Competition and ask them to underwrite it for a specific amount. In this manner, money should never be a problem.)

III. THE POINT STRUCTURE

Since the goal is fresh growth, the point structure is weighted in that direction. We give 1,000 points for every first-time visitor. Then give 2,000 points for every one of those visitors that the team gets to return to youth group the second time. (It does not need to be necessarily the very next week.) We give 3,000 points for everyone who returns a third time, and 5,000 points for everyone who returns a fourth time. The reason we do this is to create a habit. Thus, if a guest returns to your group on a repeated basis, you have a very good chance of having this person become a regular part of your group.

In order to reward the faithfulness of your individuals who are already attending, we give 1,000 points each week for every *regular* present. (*Regulars* are all attendees who are not in the visitor category. After a visitor completes their four-week attendance, they count as a regular and the group begins to get 1,000 points each week for them if they return.) Also, you cannot allow points to be given for a million things. Keep the point system simple so you reach your goal.

IV. THE LEADERSHIP STRUCTURE

Each team needs to have a core group of leaders. We use a key male and key female to run the group (college-and-career age or adult). Then we match them with key teenagers from the group to serve as assistant leaders.

Two key principles are important as you put together your leadership teams:

1) Divide up your sharper kids so one group does not begin with an obvious advantage. Explain to your teams as you formulate them that you appreciate that they are mature enough to handle not always being with their close friends. Explain that it is vital that we all understand the mission and purpose for The Great Commission Competition. The real purpose is not to win a trip (though we all want to be energized and enthusiastic about that). The real purpose is to build the kingdom of God. Thus, we cannot just leave best friends and buddies together. We want this to be more than "Christian clique time." We want to divide and conquer!

2) Try to keep most of the kids you place on a team within a two-year span of each other (like seniors and juniors, etc.). To place teams together with too wide of an age span will create tougher motivation needs. Obviously, your core leadership team may or may not be within that two-year span.

The ideal leadership team for each of your group

would be one key male leader and one key female. However, realizing that you may not have enough sharp guys to run all your teams, sometimes when you have a really sharp woman, she is all right to "fly alone" without a male counterpart. You also need between two and five "assistants." Create your own titles for them.

V. HOW DO YOU LAUNCH THE GREAT COMMISSION COMPETITION?

Step #1: Determine the number of teams you will have.

Determine the number of teams you will have. This may rise and fall on the number of leaders you have available. It will also be controlled by the number of students you have. The ideal numbers would be one team for approximately every 8–15 students that you have attending the group. (If your group is smaller, make teams of five.)

Step #2: Choose key leaders.

Choose key leaders (captains) and talk to them alone first. Sell them on the importance of just loving teenagers, and tell them this only lasts for three months. Explain that you would love to have them stay on in the ministry with you after the three months, but they are not obligated. Ask them to give it a try for these three months and leave an eternal dent on hell by helping to see kids come to Christ.

Step #3: Choose key assistants.

The "assistants" you choose to go with each team are usually quality students. They may not necessarily be tremendous Christians at this point, but they are students who are looked to as leaders and who are needed to help the momentum go in a positive fashion. (Though they may not be "tremendous Christians," my personal feeling is that they do need to be Christians.)

Step #4: Divide your group into teams.

Mentally begin to divide up the remaining students in your youth group onto teams. Start your lists and work with them for quite a while, making sure that you have enough quality people in each group for it to go well. It is fine to ask your leaders for written preference of some people they would love to have in their group (if they know any). Prepare them for the fact that if there is too much duplication of requests, they may not get their requests fulfilled.

Privately, let your leadership teams look at the team lists once they have been compiled to see if any changes need to be made. (Be sure to do this step before you go public with the team listings.)

Leadership teams need to determine a name for their teams so a sense of identity can be created pretty early in this process. (You as the leader may want to have them clear the names through you to make sure the names are sharp.)

When formulating the team lists, be sure you put names and correct phone numbers. Phone contacts become key. Work with your team leaders on what to say when they call people.

You may consider giving each team a "prospect list" with the names of other possible candidates for the youth group that do not attend. These names can be former attendees, teenagers who come on Sunday morning but not to the youth services, etc. This should be divided and given with phone numbers.

A key note: tell leaders that everyone has to stay away from each other's prospect list for one month. After that time, the names on the entire prospect list are published and open game for all leadership teams. Obviously, these become great leads and help to jump-start the competition. Some of your greatest additions, however, will come from the friends your teenagers will invite who have never darkened the door of a church facility.

Step #5: Prepare your team leaders.

Prioritize motivation with your leaders before you introduce this to the total youth group. Tell them that their excitement will make or break this whole thing. Encourage them to remember that we are all doing this to see fresh people come to Christ. Thus, we want motivational competition which remains positive, not negative.

Talk through with your leadership team any possible negatives or complaints that people will have so they know how to answer them. (For example, "I don't think we should do this because Christians shouldn't get a prize for asking people to church!" Please remind them that there will even be a reward system in heaven.)

Also, tell everyone that the points will be kept a guarded secret (even from the leaders). But if, in the first month, one team gets so obviously ahead that everyone else loses motivation, ask to be able to divide that team in the first few weeks so the overall goals of the competition do not die due to loss of motivation in the other teams.

Step #6: Determine how you will collect points.

I suggest a simple group time each week for about 10 minutes and a simple form that everyone in the group fills out at this time. (Group time is usually in the middle of the youth service because it gives the leaders time to greet visitors warmly and motivate the group to keep going.) Create a simple sheet that everyone can fill out during that group time; each group must have a specific secretary who collects the sheets and tallies the weekly results onto another pre-prepared form. Each secretary turns everything in that night to a preselected "keeper of the points" before leaving.

Again, it is vital that this information remains absolutely private, or motivation is lost very quickly.

These forms will also provide great follow-up for you because you can request visitor names and addresses. Obviously, a letter, call, or card from the leader's office is great. The main follow-up, though, is done over the phone by various members of the group making calls to the visitors. Anyone in the group can help with the follow-up. However, I suggest that you place the main "follow-up ball" in the camp of your leadership teams. Obviously, you must motivate them toward genuine friendship evangelism. Keep calling!

VI. HOW DO YOU PRESENT THIS TO THE GROUP?

Remember that the way in which you and your leadership team positively present this to the group will be very crucial. Thus, plan a night when you can launch this evangelism effort. Make the whole night around the idea of reaching out to others. Explain the Great Commission Competition (or anything you choose to name it), and do something fun like a skit or slide show (or both) to announce the prize trip. Stress that we are going to have fun, Christian competition, but that our obvious motive is to bring people to the youth group, so they can eventually come to know Christ.

End with a great time of prayer and commitment. You may want to announce the teams that night and let them gather together for a few minutes in the middle of the service so the leaders can motivate their group (i.e. "We are so glad we are together"; "We are going to have the best group").

When you announce the teams, be sure to preface it with comments like, *"Thank you for being mature enough not to whine if you are not placed with all your best friends. We are trying for the next three months to reach out and build the kingdom of God, so we do not want to be a bunch of Christian cliques. When we announce your group, please act excited! Your team leaders are in a pretty scary position because if you act like you don't want to be with them, it will make them feel pretty rotten.*

So please be mature enough to be positive when I announce your teams."

Make sure you announce that you have a special outreach night planned for the first week of the competition. Do not expect to have your kids bring people to the service if they are going to be ashamed of it. Work with your leadership teams to make this first night really special. Plan the entire three months of services realizing that you want them to be something that your kids will not be ashamed to ask their friends to attend.

As far as your trip, please also realize that you do not have to plan something for the exact end of the three months. You do need to be able to fulfill your promise within six weeks of the conclusion of the competition. Pre-think what you are going to do about students who join the winning group as the competition goes along. We usually told them that they were welcome to come on the trip, but we prorated the cost to them. (For example, if they became a part of the winning group in the last month, we paid for one-third of their trip but asked them to pay for two-thirds since the competition lasts for three months.)

VII. CLOSING COMMENTS AND PAST RESULTS

As the leader, realize that negative, superspiritual people will always have a reason why what you are doing will not work. Just kindly keep your motivation high and realize that people are people. Do not fall into the trap of allowing negative people to mess things up for everyone else.

In previous ministry groups, this simple activity usually increased our attendance (even after the conclusion of the competition) by about 33 percent. Most youth ministries that have tried something similar to this, after my suggestion, report that they have had huge, sustained growth. This approach is especially effective in sustaining growth because you create a habit for people to invite their friends to youth group. Another good thing about this approach is that it works with a very small group and with a large one.

This competition gives your kids an easy excuse to invite their friends without sounding all spiritual: "Could you come to youth group with me this week? We have a great thing going on called the Great Commission Competition. You could even come with us on our trip if our group wins. Besides, I think you'll like my youth group. Would you come with me this week?"

The other joy of this effort is that it can easily become a launching pad for small group ministry in your youth group if you desire it to be. People will become addicted to the work of the ministry, and you will find some incredible leaders coming out of the process. I wish you God's best!

May these months together be a fun-filled catalyst that sparks growth, excitement, and spiritual revival among your youth group. Indeed, new faces have a way of getting everyone and everything pretty charged up!

"The Great Commission Competition" is written by Jeanne Mayo and originally published and copyrighted by Youth Source. It is reprinted with permission. To contact Jeanne and Youth Source, please call 404.284.8262 or visit them on the web at www.youthsource.com <http://www.youthsource.com/>.

Permission to reprint "The Great Commission Competition" is limited to print rights only for *Double Vision* by Ron Luce. All other rights and permissions must be granted separately.

Jeanne reserves the right to use "The Great Commission Competition" in possible upcoming books or any other forums she may so choose without having to obtain permission from Ron Luce.

NOTES

NOTES

NOTES

NOTES

NOTES

NOTES